He Walked in Galilee

THE DAYS OF JESUS' MINISTRY

Stan Purdum

ABINGDON PRESS
NASHVILLE

HE WALKED IN GALILEE
THE DAYS OF JESUS' MINISTRY

Copyright © 2005 by Abingdon Press

All rights reserved.

No part of this work may be reproduced or transmitted in any form or by any means, electronic or mechanical, including photocopying and recording, or by any information storage or retrieval system, except as may be expressly permitted by the 1976 Copyright Act or in writing from the publisher. Requests for permission should be addressed to Abingdon Press, P.O. Box 801, 201 Eighth Avenue South, Nashville, TN 37202-0801, or permissions@abingdonpress.com.

This book is printed on acid-free paper.

Library of Congress Cataloging in Publication Data

Purdum, Stan, 1945-
    He walked in Galilee : the days of Jesus' ministry / Stan Purdum.
        p. cm.
    ISBN 0-687-00151-X (binding: adhesive perfect, pbk. : alk. paper)
    1. Jesus Christ—Biography—Public life—Meditations. 2. Jesus Christ—Example—Meditations. 3. Christian life—Meditations. 4. Christian life—Methodist authors. I. Title.

    BT340.P87 2005
    232.9'5—dc22

                                                    2004025752

Scripture quotations unless otherwise noted are from the *New Revised Standard Version of the Bible*, copyright © 1989, Division of Christian Education of the National Council of the Churches of Christ in the United States of America. Used by permission. All rights reserved.

Scripture quotations marked (CEV) are from the Contemporary English Version © 1991, 1992, 1995 by American Bible Society. Used by Permission.

First prayer page 50 is from Service of Word and Table II © 1972, 1980, 1985, 1989 The United Methodist Publishing House.

Second prayer page 50 is from Service of Word and Table © 1957 Board of Publication, Evangelical United Brethren Church © 1964, 1965, 1989 United Methodist Publishing House.

Poem page 66 is excerpted from "I Stand By the Door" [Poem by Sam Shoemaker] from I STAND BY THE DOOR: THE LIFE OF SAM SHOEMAKER by HELEN SMITH SHOEMAKER. Copyright © 1967 by Helen Smith Shoemaker. Reprinted by permission of HarperCollins Publishers Inc.

05 06 07 08 09 10 11 12 13 14 – 10 9 8 7 6 5 4 3 2 1

MANUFACTURED IN THE UNITED STATES OF AMERICA

Julia Holscher

Contents

Introduction

The most important figure on a tombstone, so common wisdom says, is the dash between the departed's date of birth and date of death. What we mean, of course, is that how the time between those two dates was spent is the real measure of a person's life.

True as the above observation is, Jesus' life was an exception. His birth was the incarnation of God; and his death, coupled with his subsequent resurrection, was redemptive for humankind. The church year is designed with the birth and death/resurrection of Jesus as its two high points—Christmas and Holy Week/Easter. So, in Jesus' case, it cannot be said that the dash is more important than what is on either side of it.

Yet, how Jesus spent the time between those two high points is significant. Much of what we know about the practice of a life faithful to God emanates from the human life Jesus lived.

This study book looks at a portion of the time indicated by that dash, the time between Jesus' baptism and the beginning of his final journey toward Jerusalem, where the cross awaited him. This period is a cohesive unit of Jesus' life, the time of his public ministry. He "went public" shortly after his baptism and the period of temptation. As Luke stated it, "Then Jesus, filled with the power of the Spirit, returned to Galilee, and a report about him spread through all the surrounding country" (Luke

4:14). Jesus remained in public view, teaching and healing, until he "set his face to go to Jerusalem" (Luke 9:51). After that point, though he did not disappear from the public eye, his mission became less to teach the crowds and more to prepare his disciples for the agony to come (for example, Matthew 20:17-19).

Because the days of Jesus' public ministry had an outward focus, it makes sense to consider the themes that marked them—to use that period to grasp Jesus as a man of his time and to try to see him as the crowds saw him. Still, there is a more personal reason as well: For many of us, glimpsing the daily life of Jesus makes it easier for us to relate to him in our daily lives. Preachers often urge us to "have a personal relationship with Jesus," but with which aspect of his life can we most easily connect? Christmas introduces us to a holy infant, Holy Week introduces us to a dying martyr. Easter introduces us to a risen Savior. The days of his ministry, however, introduce us to a man, living and teaching and loving in the full vigor of an active life. For many of us, learning more about the days of Jesus' ministry means deepening our relationship with him. My prayer is that this study book will help you to do exactly that.

In that regard, let me urge you to keep your Bible beside this book. In discussing major themes from the days of Jesus' ministry, I have tried to draw carefully and accurately from the biblical record. For that reason, I have purposely kept the book, chapter, and verse references in the text rather than in footnotes. I encourage you to take the time to locate and read the cited verses as well as the contexts in which they are found, so that you can judge for yourself what this man was about as he walked in Galilee during the days of his ministry—and what that mission means for us who seek to walk with him today.

Jesus Lived Up to His Baptism

Matthew 3:13-17

As a pastor, I love baptizing people into the Christian family of God. So imagine how happy I was one Sunday morning when I stood by the baptismal font in our church with three infants and two small boys awaiting baptism. Each baby was in the arms of a parent, and each child was standing beside his parents. There we were: one pastor, ten parents, and five little ones.

When we came to the point in the ritual for the actual baptisms, I began with the babies, taking each one in turn in my arms, sprinkling water on their heads, and pronouncing the appropriate words: "I baptize you in the name of the Father and of the Son and of the Holy Spirit." Since the two older children were too big for me to hold, I asked the parents to have each boy step forward in turn.

Completing the baptism of the third baby, I handed her back to her mother and turned toward the first of the older children, a boy of three. He took one look at me and then shouted, "Not me!" Immediately, he bolted for the back door of the sanctuary. His father, fortunately, was faster and apprehended the little fellow before he could make good his getaway. Locking the boy in his arms, the father, in the presence of the now broadly grinning congregation, marched to the front and presented his son for baptism into the kingdom of God. I then wasted no time in getting it accomplished.

On later thought, it occurred to me that maybe this young man was not greatly wrong to try to escape baptism. Far from being a harmless little ceremony, baptism begins a lifetime commitment to God, which over the long haul is no easy thing. Baptism lays on us the responsibility to live up to the vows we or our parents have made.

Jesus also had a baptism to live up to.

Jesus Baptized by John

Since Matthew (3:13-17), Mark (1:9-11), and Luke (3:21-22) each recount Jesus' baptism in some detail and John (1:32-34) alludes to it, it is obvious that all four Gospel writers understood that it signaled something of importance—but what? For centuries, readers of the Gospels have asked that question; they have wondered why Jesus chose to be baptized.

Their questioning springs from the fact that John the Baptist offered "a baptism of repentance for the forgiveness of sins" (Mark 1:4; see also Matthew 3:11; Luke 1:76-77; 3:7-8) and Jesus was without sin (2 Corinthians 5:21; 1 Peter 2:22; 1 John 3:5). Therefore, there was nothing for which Jesus needed to repent. Indeed, in Matthew's account of Jesus' baptism, John the Baptist expresses the same perplexity. When Jesus presents himself to John at the Jordan, John tries to dissuade him. "I need to be baptized by you," John says to Jesus, "and do you come to me?" (Matthew 3:14).

Jesus' response to John, while indicating that the baptism should proceed, does not completely address our bafflement. Jesus said, "Let it be so now; for it is proper for us in this way to fulfill all righteousness" (3:15). Our problem is not a difficulty in understanding the words. We know that *proper* as used here means "fitting" or "appropriate" and that *fulfill* implies "to do" or "to bring into actuality." We know too that *righteousness*, especially when it comes from the lips of Jesus, means more than being morally upright; it refers to a way of life that is faithful to God's will. So when the words are strung together in the order that Jesus used them, they mean something like, "For now this is how it should be, because we must do all that God wants us to do" (which is how the *Contemporary English Version* interprets Jesus' statement).

Our puzzlement remains, however, because we are left asking, "If Jesus' baptism was God's will, why did God want it?" Why did the Father in heaven want the sinless, holy Son of God to undergo a baptism of *repentance*? Nothing in the text answers that question for us. Yet that has not kept students of the Bible from offering theories about God's intent. In the fourth century, some persons argued that up until the moment of baptism, Jesus had no divine nature. At the baptism, divinity came upon him. This view was rejected by a church council at Nicea in A.D. 25, but the idea continues to be accepted by some Christians.

More helpfully, some Bible students have viewed Jesus' baptism as a way of his accepting, not his divine identity, but his divine task. The words the heavenly voice spoke, "This is my Son, the Beloved, with whom I am well pleased" (Matthew 3:17), combines phrases from Psalm 2:7 and Isaiah 42:1, both of which had been applied to the expected Messiah. Thus, Jesus' baptism can be viewed as a kind of ordination, the moment when he "took up his cross." While this interpretation has merit—especially when we recall that the baptism each of us has received includes the call to serve God faithfully—it puts aside the emphasis on repentance and assigns a new meaning to the act of baptism. There is no hint in the text, however, that Jesus expected his baptism to be for a different purpose than everybody else's baptism; and as the Son of God, he surely already knew his mission, though this may have been the moment when he embraced it.

Another view says that by undergoing a baptism of repentance, Jesus was putting himself in solidarity with all who need to repent and who thus are under God's judgment. In this view, Jesus' repentance is on behalf of all he came to save. To say it differently, he took sin on, not to become a participant in it, but to share the weight of it.

Or, it is also possible that for Jesus, as for many of us who seek baptism, the act was one of dedication, regardless of any need for repentance. Though Jesus was fully divine, he was also fully human (as the fact that he faced temptations immediately following his baptism shows); so "to fulfill all righteousness," Jesus had to take his human nature in hand and to offer it unreservedly to God.

As the variety of these possible explanations suggests, our questions about the meaning of Jesus' baptism cannot be answered unequivocally. What we can know for certain, however, is that in submitting himself to the baptism of repentance, Jesus did the will of God. The proof of that fact is that as the baptism was completed, the Spirit of God descended on Jesus. God used the occasion not only to make an announcement regarding Jesus' divine identity but also to state God's unqualified approval of him.

From reading the accounts of Jesus' baptism in Matthew, Mark, and Luke, it is not clear that anyone other than Jesus himself heard the words of the voice from heaven, although the wording in Matthew is "*This* is my Son" (3:17, italics added) rather than "*You* are my Son." Also, in John's Gospel, the Baptist says that he "saw the Spirit descending from heaven like a dove" (1:32), so presumably John also heard the voice. In the end though, it does not matter who else heard the words; for Jesus arose from that experience with the inner confirmation of the path he was to follow.

"I Am Baptized"

We who read the Gospels may continue to wonder about the theological significance of Jesus' baptism, but this much is obvious from the Scriptures: Jesus went on from that point to live a life that showed the marks of his divine call and blessing. In other words, he lived up to his baptism.

During Martin Luther's great struggle to reform the church in the sixteenth century, when the Holy Roman Emperor was seeking to silence him, he spent some lonely months in

Wartburg Castle under protective custody. There, as he fought despair, he scribbled the words "I am baptized" on his desktop as a reminder that he was living according to an ongoing call from God. He did not write "I *was* baptized" but used the present tense verb. Luther rightly understood that in his baptism, he had not merely undergone a one-time liturgical rite but had accepted God's call to follow—for the rest of his life—the path God placed before him. Later, in his *Large Catechism*, Luther wrote that "to be baptized in God's name is to be baptized not by human beings but by God himself. Although it is performed by human hands, it is nevertheless truly God's own act." [1]

Two centuries later, John Wesley, the founder of Methodism, emphasized the continuing nature of baptism when he wrote, "By baptism we enter into covenant with God; into that everlasting covenant, which he hath commanded for ever."[2]

Jesus lived up to his baptism, and we should live up to ours. I heard about a man who purchased a home sight unseen. When asked why he was willing to take such a chance, he explained, "I know the man who built it, and he builds Christianity in with the bricks." Whether or not that builder consciously recalled his baptism as he went about his work I do not know, but he was living up to his baptism nonetheless.

Sometimes living up to our baptism is easy and perhaps even pleasurable and rewarding. Other times though, it might be more convenient not to have been baptized.

One of the churches I pastored was in a rural county in northeast Ohio that was composed of several small townships, none too heavily populated. Like most of the churches in those townships, my congregation put some money aside to help people in need, a fund that I as pastor administered. Thus, it was not uncommon to find people at my door requesting help to purchase food or baby supplies or other items. For the most part, these were people I knew; but sometimes, the requests for help came by telephone. In those cases, it was usually from someone I did not know. These were often people who had gotten help so frequently from the church nearest them that they were now being turned away, and so they were "prospecting" to find other sources of aid. Some had legitimate needs, but others were working the system. It was always difficult for pastors to tell one from the other.

One Friday evening, when I was particularly tired and looking forward to a restful evening at home, I received a call from a woman in a township fifteen miles away. At least four other churches were nearer to her than ours, so I assumed that she had exhausted all their resources and was now reaching out further. She had such a tale to tell—hungry children in her house and an inability to reach anyone at any of the churches nearer to her home. My internal "bogus story" meter was going off, but of course, I could not be sure. Also, since it was Friday night, the county welfare office was closed. Calling there to check her need or to see if she really had any children was not an option.

My immediate inclination was to say no; but then, suppose her story was true. If there really were hungry children in the house, they should not suffer because of their parents' misfortune, lack of planning, or other circumstances. So I finally agreed to give the woman a food voucher to use at her local supermarket. I told her I would have it ready for her to pick up.

She then said that she had no transportation. Could I deliver it? A thirty-mile round trip, mind you. I was about to say no when, for some reason, the fact of my baptism popped into my mind. I remembered that I am—not just *have been* but *am*—baptized. *I am baptized!* My baptism acknowledges that I *am*—not just *have been* or *am when it is convenient*—a child of God. That means my behavior is a reflection on God. Realizing that, I had to ask myself what ought I to do that would reflect rightly on him?

You know the answer. That Friday evening, it certainly would have been more convenient for me *not* to be baptized; but I am. Baptism is not something we can take off like clothing that has gotten uncomfortable. I made the delivery.

When I drove into the woman's driveway, there were four vehicles sitting there and I found no children in the house. They were all out with their father at that moment, the woman said, which of course begged the question of what *he* was using for transportation. Probably she was working the system—though from the look of her place, her poverty was real enough.

For me, whether she deserved help or not was beside the point. I needed to live up to my baptism and I have never regretted that I did.

The Baptismal Choice

John the Baptist offered a baptism of repentance. When we seek baptism (or, for those of us baptized as children, seek confirmation), there is the implication that we are making a choice about the kind of people we intend to be. Among the Amish, this is put into a specific lifestyle context; for prior to the time Amish young people undergo baptism and become full members of their sect, there is a period called *rumschpringes* ("running around"). Because they are not yet baptized, the sect's strict rules do not yet apply; and some of the youth use this period to try out the ways of the world. Although eighty to eighty-five percent of these young people eventually choose baptism and embrace the ways of their people and of the Christian faith, some do not. A few even get into deep trouble. In 1998, for example, two Amish young men were charged with dealing cocaine. While we cannot know all that was in their hearts, we can say this: Had they chosen baptism and all that it implies, they would not have pursued the direction they did.

While few of us see baptism as involving living without modern conveniences as do the Amish, the choice to be baptized nonetheless involves other lifestyle and life-spending decisions. In 1935, the wives of Spanish-speaking pastors of Methodist churches held a meeting in Mission, Texas. Due to family illnesses, neither the president nor the vice-president was able to be at the meeting. Angelina Moraida, the secretary, had also been seriously ill, but because she lived nearby, she made the effort to come and preside at the meeting. She arrived feeling poorly and it was hard on her to carry out her duties. Many attendees urged her to go home, but Angelina replied,

"As long as there is breath of life in me, the women's work of this conference will go on." While she did not phrase her commitment in terms of baptism, her remark had definite overtones of the "I am baptized" spirit. One woman who overheard that comment was a young clergy wife who had been trying to sort out her place in the church. Two weeks later, Angelina Moraida died from her illness, and this young wife, inspired by Angelina's commitment, offered herself to do what she could for the church. In other words, by viewing Angelina's determination to live up to her baptism, this young woman found the answer to her search. She may have hoped for some other answer, something easier, but what she heard from God was, "Be as committed to me as Angelina was."

This young woman's name was Clotilde Falcón Náñez. She went on to earn a master's degree and had a long career teaching English to non-English–speaking people. She also served the church for twenty-six years by translating women's program books into Spanish. Her incentive for choosing that path for her life was the faithfulness of a baptized Christian, Angelina Moraida. [3]

Living Wet

It would be incorrect to suggest that living up to one's baptism always means doing difficult things or things we would not be inclined to do otherwise. It does mean that the memory of one's baptism should be a guide to how we live every day. Living the baptized life has sometimes been called "living wet"; and that "wetness" can coalesce into a shower of blessing on us, as well as on others.

My personal history puts me in a position to talk about the difference baptism makes. Although I grew up in a Christian family and made a personal decision to follow Christ when I was twelve, I was not baptized until I was twenty. The church of my youth was The Salvation Army, a denomination that does not baptize its members. They are not opposed to baptism, but since they view the sacrament as symbolic of a person's acceptance of God's grace through Christ, they focus on urging that acceptance rather than on the ritual of baptism. They work toward inner baptism but do not use any outward rite to signify it.

When I was an infant, my parents had me dedicated in our local Salvation Army corps (church), a service similar to infant baptism but with no water used. Later, when I made my own decision for Christ, I experienced a change of direction that caused me to consider everything I did thereafter in light of my commitment to Christ. I believe that was an inner baptism.

At age twenty, a series of circumstances led me to seek membership in The Methodist Church. As part of the membership preparation, the pastor explained the requirement for baptism. While I agreed to be baptized, I approached it with the idea that it was just a symbol of a commitment I had made a few years earlier. The pastor made no attempt to dissuade me of that view. In fact, he explained that Methodist teaching does not claim that actual forgiveness of sins and spiritual rebirth happens at the moment the water is applied. He also agreed that the outward "sign" was to signify an inward commitment. Nonetheless, he said, baptism would be an important milestone in my ongoing experience of Christ.

Actually, when the day of my baptism came, though I approached it reverently, I did not feel anything new happen. The ritual proceeded, and a few days later, I joined the church. That pastor was right, however, about the importance of that baptism service. As time went on, I found that remembering my baptism became an important means of deciding how I would behave in given situations—including the one I described earlier about the woman seeking assistance. It also served as a reminder that I belong to Christ.

In a denomination that offers infant baptism, it is important to give those baptized at a young age an opportunity to have that milestone experience that my baptism as a young adult provided me. Wisely, such churches do this with confirmation. That is the ritual, usually preceded by weeks of study of church doctrines and history, whereby persons confirm the promises made at their baptism, whether they made the promises themselves or their parents made them on their behalf. I have always liked how one such ritual words the confirmation question: "Do you here, in the presence of God, and of this congregation, renew the solemn promise and vow that you made, or that was made in your name, at your Baptism?"[4] A later similar ritual includes the same concept in the pastor's opening statements as "Through confirmation...we renew the covenant declared at our baptism."[5] If we were baptized when too young to make the promise for ourselves, confirmation is the public declaration that we are taking them on and that we are called to live up to them.

The concept that the Christian life is "living wet" shows up in another ritual as well. A service titled "Congregational Reaffirmation of the Baptismal Covenant," includes the instruction that it is to be used "when there are no candidates to be baptized, confirmed, or received into membership."[6] The purpose of the ritual, as the title suggests, is to help participants remember and again say yes to their baptismal vows. Though no one is rebaptized, water is used in other symbolic ways. For example, the pastor can "scoop up a handful of water and let it flow back into the font so that it is heard and seen," can "touch the water and mark each person on the forehead with the sign of the cross," or use some similar method.[7]

The point of each of these rituals, of course, is that baptism lays on us the same privilege and call it placed on Jesus—to do the will of God.

The Baptism of the Cross

We also acknowledge that for Jesus there was an added element that is not placed upon us by our baptism. He was called to be the centerpiece of the greatest salvation action of all time, an action that was fulfilled on the cross. Jesus indicated that going to the cross was part of his baptismal call when, in response to the request of James and John to have the chief places with him in glory, he said, "You do not know what you are asking. Are you able to drink the cup that I drink, or be baptized with the baptism that I am baptized with?" (Mark 10:38). Here, "cup" and "baptism" are metaphors for the suffering and death Jesus was soon to face. Thus, for him, living up to his baptism ultimately meant going to the cross. At times, of course, living up to our baptism could mean something similar for us. When James and John both asserted in response to Jesus' question, "We are able," Jesus said to them, "The cup that I drink you will drink; and with the baptism with which I am baptized, you will be baptized" (Mark 10:39). In James's case, that was literally true. According to Acts 12:1-2, James was later slain by King Herod for being part of the church. While we do not know how his brother John died, we do know that John remained an active part of the church through the persecutions and surely until his death, however it came.

The Baptism Resurrection

Baptism may be performed using the method called "sprinkling," where a small amount of water is placed on the person's head directly from the pastor's hand. Pastors can also baptize by "pouring," in which water is literally poured over the person's head. Further, pastors can use the "immersion" method, in which the person is put fully beneath water in either an indoor tank or outdoors in a natural body of water. Since baptism is a symbolic action, the amount of water used is not of primary importance.

There is, however, something to be said for the immersion method: Because it is the only one that involves the threat of drowning and sudden deliverance from death, it is a direct reminder that when we are baptized, we put to death all within us that is opposed to Christ and are "resurrected" out of the water as a new person committed to "living wet" as his disciple.

Actually, that commitment should happen in the heart beforehand, with the baptism following to symbolize the inner commitment. Whenever one's baptism takes place, from that point onward, we, like Jesus, have a baptism to live up to.

Study Guide

1. In what ways was John the Baptist right about his needing what Jesus could give? In what ways was Jesus right about his needing what John could give?

2. Of the possible explanations for Jesus' baptism described in this chapter, which one makes the most sense to you? Why?

3. In what sense was your baptism, or confirmation of the baptismal vows made for you by others, an act of repentance?

4. Think of a time when you would have preferred not to have the obligation your baptismal promises bring. How did you handle the situation?

5. What joys are associated with your baptism?

6. According to Matthew 28:19, Jesus' final words to his followers included not only instructions to teach his commands and make disciples in all nations but also to baptize them "in the name of the Father and of the Son and of the Holy Spirit." Why do you think Jesus made baptism just as important as disciple-making and Gospel-teaching?

Notes

1. *Large Catechism*, IV:10, Kolb/Wengert, 457. Quoted by John T. Pless, "I Am Baptized: What Does This Mean?" www.lifeoftheworld.com/lotw/06-02/06-02-04.php.

2. "A Treatise on Baptism," *The Works of the Rev. John Wesley, A.M., with Last Corrections of the Author.* Quoted by Robert W. Burtner and Robert E. Chiles, *A Compend of Wesley's Theology* (New York: Abingdon Press, 1954), p. 266.

3. Hilah F. Thomas and Rosemary Skinner Keller, eds, *Women in New Worlds: Historical Perspectives on the Wesleyan Tradition*, Volume 1 (Nashville: Abingdon Press, 1981), pp. 170-71. The book is a collection of papers presented at a women's conference in Cincinnati in 1980. Clotilde Falcón Náñez was the author of chapter 8.

4. *The Book of Worship for Church and Home* (Nashville: The Methodist Publishing House, 1964), p. 12.

5. "The Baptismal Covenant I," *The United Methodist Hymnal* (Nashville, The United Methodist Publishing House, 1989), p. 33.

6. "The Baptismal Covenant IV," *The United Methodist Hymnal*, pp. 50-53.

7. *The United Methodist Book of Worship* (Nashville: The United Methodist Publishing House, 1992), pp. 113-14.

Session 2

JESUS PROCLAIMED
THE GOOD NEWS OF GOD

Mark 1:9-15

Life presents us with any number of vitally important opportunities for new understanding, but it is awfully easy to miss the point. One of those opportunities came at a conference in Detroit aimed especially at men with daughters. The event, sponsored by "Dads Empowered," was a response to the abundant research that shows that girls who have a close relationship with their fathers are less likely to behave promiscuously, develop eating disorders, drop out of school, or commit suicide. That means that while their daughters are still young, fathers should make extra efforts to bond with them.

The seminar helped the fathers examine what sort of messages they were giving their daughters when they leered at a woman or commented on a woman's weight or appearance. The session leader said that a lot of girls have a distorted view of themselves, fostered in part by the sexual messages in the culture and the load of negative feedback they receive from cliques and bullies. "We have a lot of girls walking around saying mean things to themselves: 'I'm fat. I'm ugly. I'm stupid,' " the conference leader said. In the face of this, a father can do a lot to help by reminding his daughter of her strengths.

Men need to understand the power of small rituals of support that telegraph to their daughters, "Dad cares about me." After attending the conference, one father decided to put a note in his eleven-year-old daughter's lunch. It read, "Have a great day! Love, Dad." The daughter was so touched by it that she wrote her father a full-page letter thanking him and asking for more messages in her lunches.

Seeing how much this little gesture meant to his child, the man told three coworkers, all fathers, about the incident. One of these fathers responded, "Great idea. I'll have my wife do it." [1]

You see how easy it is to miss the point? Many of the most important things we need to know in life are stated quietly or come when we are not paying attention, and we can miss them.

The Good News

The heart of the message Jesus proclaimed came in a similar way—or at least that is how it seems when reading the Gospel of Mark. That Gospel is the shortest of the four, and it is also the one that moves the story of Jesus along most quickly. Mark does not include a birth story but opens with John the Baptist announcing the arrival on the scene of the adult Jesus. There is a breathless quality to Mark—this happened, then this, then this—bang, bang, bang.

In Mark 1:9-15 (seven verses), for example, we are told about the baptism of Jesus by John, Jesus' temptations in the wilderness, the arrest of John, and Jesus' arrival in Galilee soon afterward. There, Jesus preached "the good news of God."

In verses 14-15, Mark states the essence of Jesus' message—that which he spent his time on earth delivering: "Now after John was arrested, Jesus came to Galilee, proclaiming the good news of God, and saying, 'The time is fulfilled, and the kingdom of God has come near; repent, and believe in the good news.'"

There are not many words in these verses; but if we rush by them, we may miss the point. Brief though they are, these lines tell of two momentous indicators that a dramatic change had taken place and of two calls for action that people should take as a result. Or as one commentator puts it, there are two "facts" and two "acts" in these verses. [2]

Notice first, though, that Mark reported that Jesus came

announcing "the good news of God." When Mark opened his book, his first sentence was, "The beginning of the good news of Jesus Christ, the Son of God." He looked at the life and work of Jesus and called it "good news," which is what the word *gospel* means. Note also that when Jesus came, he did not point to himself—though he was part of the good news—but to the work of God, which he rightly called good news.

The content of that news is contained in the two facts given in Mark 1:14-15.

The Time Is Fulfilled

The first fact is, "the time is fulfilled." This was a way of saying that the period of waiting was over. We know from the Old Testament that many of the Jewish people were looking for a new action from God, an intervention in the course of history that would change things dramatically. The focal point of this new action was the hope for a Messiah, a savior who would come and rescue the people from their domination by the Roman Empire and lead them to new heights of security, peace, and glory.

The term *messiah* means "anointed one." Anointing, the pouring of oil over the head of a person, was a rite used to designate formally and publicly that person as having been chosen by God for a specific task or role. Anointing was used, for example, to commission a high priest. Psalm 133:2 gives a vivid picture of the anointing of Aaron for this position:

> It is like the precious oil on the head,
> running down upon the beard,
> on the beard of Aaron,
> running down over the collar of his robes.

And that before the days of dry cleaning!

When God selected David to be king, the prophet Samuel was instructed to seek David out. "Then Samuel took the horn of oil, and anointed [David] in the presence of his brothers"

(1 Samuel 16:13). It was far more than a mere human ceremony, however; for, as the rest of the verse explains, "the spirit of the LORD came mightily upon David from that day forward." The anointing was not just with oil but also with God's Spirit.

As king, David led Israel to its zenith; and during his reign, God promised David that through him and his descendants God would establish a "kingdom forever" (2 Samuel 7:12-16). As time moved on and the people's fortunes cycled gradually downward, that promise remained a rock of hope. The people clung to the promise that God would anoint another person of the line of David to redeem them from their troubles.

The prophets articulated that hope. One was Isaiah, who lived in the time after the kingdom once ruled by David had split into two kingdoms. During Isaiah's lifetime, the Assyrians destroyed the Northern Kingdom of Israel and forced its people into captivity. Isaiah was a citizen of the Southern Kingdom of Judah; and he was convinced that his homeland was soon to experience a similar fate, which it eventually did. He warned the people of what was coming but also announced that the Davidic kingdom would survive, eventually to be led by "a son given to us...and he is named...Prince of Peace" (Isaiah 9:6). Micah, who was a contemporary of Isaiah, also told of a savior to come, specifically saying that this person would be born in Bethlehem (Micah 5:2), the birthplace of David.

Years later, after the people of Judah had been exiled to Babylonia and eventually allowed to return to their homeland, the prophet who speaks in Isaiah 56–66, prophesied of one who would be anointed to deliver good news to the downtrodden (Isaiah 61:1-3). Other prophets reinforced his messianic expectation; but by the first century A.D., the Jews had been waiting for several hundred years for the fulfillment of the expectation. Then, Jesus arrived and said, "The time is fulfilled"—the time of waiting had been completed, and the era for which they had been waiting had come.

To get a sense of why this announcement is part of the good news, think of modern-day people who live in countries ruled by totalitarian dictators, where most personal freedoms are denied. In some of those countries, there are embassies of the free nations—the United States, Canada, Great Britain, and others—and in some cases, it is possible for the citizens of the repressed nation to go to one of those embassies and to apply for permission to emigrate to the free nation. That permission is not granted automatically. Even assuming there is nothing on record to mark the individual as an undesirable person, the permission is usually not forthcoming immediately. Even after it is granted, the applicant is placed on a waiting list until a slot opens in the receiving country, and sometimes that wait can amount to years. For some, though, after a long wait, the notice finally arrives from the embassy that the time for emigration has arrived. That is a day of good news. The time is fulfilled, and the person's new life is about to begin.

That experience is similar to what Jesus was saying about God's new action in the world. The time of waiting was over. In this passage, Jesus does not say that he is the Messiah; but all of the Gospel writers testify that such was the case. Luke recorded the incident in the Nazareth synagogue where Jesus read the messianic prophecy from Isaiah 61 and then told those gathered, "Today this scripture has been fulfilled in your hearing" (Luke 4:16-21).

The Kingdom of God Has Come Near

The second fact Jesus states in Mark 1:15, "The kingdom of God has come near," is a critical piece of the announcement. If Jesus had only said that the time was fulfilled, that by itself could be the beginning of bad news, not good.

To go back to our example of the person in a country under totalitarian rule waiting for permission to emigrate, the time of waiting could have ended with a notice from the embassy of the free nation stating that they had decided to deny the person entry into their country. That would be saying that the time was fulfilled but that what had come was bad news.

As another example, imagine yourself having some physical symptoms that cause concern about your health. Your doctor orders some tests, and you wait for the results. When the results finally come in, the time is fulfilled; but the news could be either bad or good.

In the case of Jesus' message, it was pure good news. Not only was the time of waiting over, but the kingdom of God had drawn near. God had come to be present among the people in a fresh and new way. God's new day was about to dawn. Something fresh was beginning with the appearance of Jesus.

Those of you who have jobs where you work under the direction of others may know what it is like to have a supervisor or a boss who is difficult or perhaps even nasty to work for. Then one day, that person is fired, retires, is promoted, dies, or in some other way leaves the job and a new person takes that position. There is a sense in which the new person brings in a new era, especially if he or she is a better supervisor, a kinder leader, one with more concern for the people being supervised. A new reign begins.

Jesus was saying something similar, only much more so. The kingdom of God meant that God was entering human history in a way that offered mortals new opportunities, new hope, new joy, new ways of thinking, and new ways of living.

With his arrival, Jesus said the kingdom had "come near." The wording of the original Greek gives the sense, not that the Kingdom was an accomplished fact, but that it had "begun to arrive." That tone of begun-but-not-fully-here continued to mark Jesus' later statements about the Kingdom as well. While he said in Mark 1:15 that with his coming the Kingdom had already begun, he later talked about the Kingdom coming in the future, with his return: "Then the sign of the Son of Man will appear in heaven, and then all the tribes of the earth will mourn, and they will see 'the Son of Man coming on the clouds of heaven' with power and great glory" (Matthew 24:30). On another occasion, Jesus was asked by the Pharisees when the kingdom of God was coming. He answered, "The kingdom of God is not coming with things that can be observed; nor will they say, 'Look, here it is!' or 'There it is!' For, in fact, the kingdom of God is *among* you" (Luke 17:20-21, italics added). Thus, both statements about the Kingdom—that it is yet to come and is already here—are true.

Certainly with Jesus' arrival in the first century, the Kingdom had begun and became present, at least in the hearts of Jesus' followers. In fact, the word translated "among" in Luke 17:21 can also be rendered as "within." That sense of the Kingdom within is also apparent in several short parables Jesus told. In them, Jesus did not describe the Kingdom. Instead, he used comparisons, similes: "The kingdom of heaven is like ..." In these parables, Jesus said the Kingdom is like a tiny seed that grows into a great tree, like a little yeast that leavens the entire day's baking, like a treasure hidden in a field, and like a pearl that a merchant wants so badly that he sells everything else he owns to purchase it (Matthew 13:31-33, 44-46).

These parables are all about the kingdom of God *within* Jesus' followers, and that includes you and me. We who follow Jesus possess the seed of the kingdom and the yeast of God's love. We have the treasure of the good news, the message that is valuable beyond all others.

Repent

This knowledge of the good news of the Kingdom leads to the two acts, the two actions we need to do to take advantage of the opportunity the kingdom of God coming near provides.

The first of these actions, said Jesus, is to *repent* (Mark 1:15). One meaning of "repent" is to turn away from our sins. That sense of the word is included here, but the original Greek word used in the text also means to shift the direction of one's life. In this case, that is a shift that causes one to give full attention to the kingdom of God. That is an important distinction. We are so used to thinking of the gospel as primarily having to do with forgiveness of sins that it would be easy for those who do not feel particularly sinful to wonder if what Jesus said has any meaning for them. Jesus said, however, that the approach of the kingdom of God is for all of us, not just those who are conscious of their sins. The Kingdom is a significant new direction for our lives.

Former Congresswoman Pat Schroeder related an experience that will help us understand the change of direction implied by repentance. In 1970, Schroeder, although a law-school graduate, was a thirty-year-old stay-at-home mother with a four-year-old son and a new baby daughter. A few days after giving birth to her daughter, Schroeder experienced a postdelivery complication that nearly killed her. In fact, she awoke in the hospital to find a priest administering last rites. In time, she recovered, but she found that she had changed in an essential way. Struck by the fragility of life, she resolved that if she saw something she thought she should do, she was "gonna jump on it."

At first, Schroeder returned to part-time employment, some involving pro bono work for human-services agencies. Then, two years later, her husband urged her to run for Congress. While that at first seemed an overwhelming idea, Schroeder said, "If not for that business in the hospital, I would have been more uptight about the consequences." As it turned out, she was elected. Later in her congressional career, that hospital experience also inspired her to lead the fight to get the Women's Health Initiative passed, legislation that is now yielding results such as research on hormone replacement therapy. [3]

Schroeder's is not a religious story per se, and you may not agree with her career decision or her politics, but the dramatic refocusing of her life caused by nearly hemorrhaging to death in 1970 illustrates a kind of repentance that is not a turning from sin but a changing of direction caused by a new mind-set.

The repentance Jesus called for often involves both a turning away from sin and a turning toward the Kingdom, but it always involves the latter. Jesus announced that the kingdom of God is at hand. A new mind-set is required to enter it.

Believe the Good News

The second action Jesus spoke of was to "believe in the good news" (Mark 1:15). To believe something in the sense implied here is not so much being convinced of a fact, the way we believe that the world is round, but *acting* on our conviction. If I believe that a certain doctor can cure me of a disease, then I demonstrate that belief by putting myself in his or her care. If I believe that the way of Jesus Christ is the best way to live, then I demonstrate that belief by trying to live my life in the way of Jesus Christ.

In addition, Jesus' call to believe implied that the time for acting was right then and, in our case, right now. There was a sense of urgency. The time of waiting was over. Time was up. Decision time had come.

To return once more to the example of a person who has applied for emigration to a free nation, this call to believe is the equivalent of the person receiving a notice that said, "Come to the embassy on Tuesday morning at 9 a.m. for the official document of permission." If you were that person and you really wanted to go to the free nation, would you say, "Well, Tuesday is not convenient; I'll go in when I get a chance"? Of course not. Jesus' call carries that same "the time to act is now" importance.

A story from the business world illustrates this point. A few years ago, when the Fox television network decided to launch a twenty-four-hour news service to compete with CNN, they lured Roger Ailes, who was then running CNBC and America's Talking (which became MSNBC) from that company to head the new news service. After Ailes made the move, eighty-two people who had been working for him at NBC left that company to join Ailes at Fox. When NBC executives complained about Ailes stealing staff, Ailes responded by saying, "You don't know the difference between recruitment and a jailbreak." [4] These were people who apparently saw a moment of opportunity to go to where they believed things would be better. An even greater sense of urgency and opportunity arises from Jesus' call to believe the good news.

The heart of the good news is not a new idea or a fresh load of guilt or a novel philosophy of life or a new code of behavior. It is a call to respond to Jesus Christ. It is a call to commit our lives to following Jesus and obeying God.

The Kingdom of God *Now*

Some of this urgency about the nearness of the Kingdom does not have meaning for us because whatever was meant by the approach of the kingdom of God two thousand years ago, it did not mean the end of human pain, suffering, injustice, or the unfairness of life. Many things have changed in the outward world since the time of Jesus, but the power of evil and greed and self-centeredness has marched on unabated.

What we have to understand is two things: First, that the *fullness* of the Kingdom will not come until the end of time, and second, the Kingdom is present powerfully in an inward way right now. People who commit their lives to Jesus Christ experience a sense of joy and peace and hope often not justified by outward circumstances. Yet, in the realm of the heart and mind, the regions where peace, joy, and hope matter most, the victory has already been won. The kingdom of God means that Jesus invites us to sign on to the winning team.

Do not misunderstand. I am not suggesting that Christianity does not care about or help the outward life as well. Christianity has always insisted that it takes all aspects of our lives—mind, body, and spirit—to make us fully human and that Christ came for all that we are in our entirety. We need to recognize, however, that in terms of how we feel about life and how we interact with life, the mind is the steering mechanism.

In his landmark book about mental and spiritual health, *The Road Less Traveled*, psychiatrist M. Scott Peck wrote, "I make no distinction between the mind and the spirit, and therefore no distinction between the process of achieving spiritual growth and achieving mental growth. They are one and the same." [5] In daily living, we do not divide ourselves into mind, body, and spirit, and there is no indication that Jesus' message about the good news did that either. Thus, the inner experience of the kingdom of God has a great bearing on all aspects of our lives *now.*

Mark tells us that Jesus came proclaiming good news. It was and is good news because it invites us to a loving relationship with God through Jesus Christ. It is good news regarding sin's grip because it testifies that God's grip is stronger. The gospel is good news because it is hopeful not only about our ultimate destiny but also about the mundane difficulties of each day. It is good news because it offers hope in the face of crises and tragedies. It is good news because the gospel both sustains us in the face of threat and empowers us to tackle insincerity, injustice, sinfulness, and other evil forces in the culture. It is good news because it breaks down barriers between people and calls us to see that we are fully related to one another because we all have the same Creator. The gospel is good news because it gives us confidence in the face of death that God waits for us beyond death. It is good news because this gospel both helps us live and helps us when we die.

In the end, the full understanding of what Jesus' good news is will come to each one of us, not by dissecting it into facts and acts, but by embracing it and discovering for ourselves why the opportunities presented by the nearness of the kingdom of God will revolutionize our lives.

Study Guide

1. What vital understandings of life did you learn in a quiet discovery? What important things had to hit you over the head to get your attention? What things have you had to keep relearning and why?

2. In what specific ways do you experience the kingdom of God in your life?

3. As pointed out, Scott Peck wrote, "I make no distinction between the mind and the spirit, and therefore no distinction between the process of achieving spiritual growth and achieving mental growth. They are one and the same." In what ways do you agree with his statement? In what ways do you disagree?

4. Read Isaiah 61:1-3. In what ways do those verses apply to Jesus?

5. What turning point kinds of experiences have you had? What new life directions resulted?

6. In what sense has your own experience of repentance been a changing of direction?

Notes

1. Jeffrey Zaslow, "Papa, Don't Preach: Why Some Fathers Don't Relate Well to Their Daughters," *The Wall Street Journal* (November 6, 2003): D1.

2. Bonnie Bowman Thurston, *Preaching Mark* (Minneapolis: Fortress Press, 2002), p. 18.

3. Pat Schroeder, "Close Call," *Time* (November 11, 2002): A14.

4. Joe Flint, "Playing the Underdog Helps Fox News Stay on Top of CNN," *The Wall Street Journal* (January 15, 2003): B1, B12.

5. M. Scott Peck, *The Road Less Traveled* (New York: Simon and Schuster, 1978), p. 11.

Session 3

JESUS HEALED THE SICK

Matthew 8:1-17

My wife, Jeanine, is both a committed Christian and a registered nurse. A few years ago, she went to Haiti with a mission team. While other team members were there to construct a school building, Jeanine went as the team nurse. When the Haitian church leaders learned that the team included a nurse, they requested that she come prepared to teach a first-aid class to clergy, and Jeanine agreed. Since the ministers spoke only Creole and Jeanine spoke only English, she had to teach the class through an interpreter; but it worked out fine.

The pastors expressed warm appreciation for what Jeanine taught them, but she also learned something—why members of the *clergy* wanted first-aid training. You might guess that it had to do with a shortage of healthcare workers in the island nation, and that was part of the reason. Mainly though, it had to do with belief. In that nation, many people follow the voodoo religion. When they are sick, they call for a witch doctor, a practitioner of that faith. When those same people hear the gospel and are converted to Christianity, they stop relying on the witch doctor for healing and turn instead to a practitioner of the Christian faith, the local pastor. Think what you will, there is a certain logic to that switch, because the converts are bringing with them a worldview in which faith and health are closely connected.

It will help us understand the electrifying effect of Jesus' arrival in first-century Palestine if we keep in mind that many of the people of Jesus' day believed essentially the same thing. They had the Hebrew Scriptures and knew, for example, of the account in 1 Kings 17 where Elijah revives the son of a widow from death. After the boy awakens, his mother says to Elijah, "Now I know that you are *a man of God*" (1 Kings 17:24, italics added). Note that she does not say, "Now I know you are a man of medicine." She linked healing with religion.

Jesus did not spend a lot of time attempting to change the view that faith and health are inseparable, but when asked directly about it, he showed a larger understanding. John 9 tells of a man who was born blind. When Jesus and his disciples happened past this man one day, the disciples asked Jesus, "Rabbi, who sinned, this man or his parents, that he was born blind?" Jesus answered, "Neither this man nor his parents sinned; he was born blind so that God's works might be revealed in him" (John 9:2-3). With that reply, Jesus indicated that the man's lack of eyesight had nothing to do with sin on anyone's part. The fact that the disciples asked the question, however, demonstrates their assumption that illness was tied to God's judgment. In that regard, they were no different from their neighbors. In fact, the link between illness and judgment continued well into the Middle Ages. It was not until the Reformation that illness was disassociated from sin and medicines could be freely used. [1]

That sickness is something the afflicted "deserve" is a notion that resurfaces repeatedly. In the late 1970s, we first learned of the disease AIDS as it affected—and initially seemed limited to—homosexual men. Among people who viewed practicing homosexuals as sinners, some wondered if the disease might not be God's punishment on that population. A few went so far as to declare it so.

A Major Activity for Jesus

By and large, most of us do not consider a person's illness or injuries a judgment from God. While that is good, it also

makes it difficult to see how Jesus' healing work in an age rid-
dled with medical ignorance has much to do with us in the
twenty-first century. Yet, as we focus on Jesus' public ministry,
one of the things we cannot escape—no matter which of the
Gospels we read—is that Jesus spent a lot of time and energy
healing people. In the four Gospels, there are more than forty
recorded instances when Jesus healed, and more than thirty of
them refer to healing from physical infirmities. Because Jesus
gave so much time to that task, we cannot dismiss it as having
no bearing on us, as if what he *said* during that is important
for the twenty-first century but not what he *did*.

Still, it is easier to see the relevance of his teachings for us
than his healing activities for two reasons. First, we live in an age
where medicine has developed as a separate discipline from religion. We have seen the miracles medicine can work. When we
have a family member who is ill, we may call the church to have
the person put on the prayer list, but that is not all we do. We
also seek professional medical care for our loved one. Second, as
Christians we have been embarrassed by revelations that several
high-profile "faith healers" were charlatans. They were not healing anyone; rather, they were fleecing their flock to make themselves rich. We want nothing to do with such scams.

Nonetheless, we cannot write off this activity of Jesus that all
four Gospel writers record. One of those writers was Luke, who
was a physician (Colossians 4:14). All the Gospels, but especially Luke, use the expression "to heal" in reference to Jesus'
mission. Note, for example, this verse: "One day, while [Jesus]
was teaching, Pharisees and teachers of the law were sitting
near by . . . ; and the power of the Lord was with him to heal"
(Luke 5:17). In another place, Luke reported that people came
to Jesus "to hear him and to be healed of their diseases" (Luke
6:18). In that context, Luke added that "power came out from
[Jesus] and healed all of them" (6:19). Luke also reported that
Jesus acknowledged healing as a necessary part of his work.
After some Pharisees warned Jesus that Herod was out to kill
him, Jesus responded, "Go and tell that fox for me, 'Listen, I am
casting out demons and performing cures today and tomorrow,
and on the third day I finish my work' " (Luke 13:32).

How Jesus Viewed Healing

To help us think about how Jesus' healing ministry applies to those who follow him today, consider these observations from the Scriptures:

1. It appears that Jesus did not consider healing his primary mission. As we pointed out in the last chapter, Jesus declared that his purpose was to proclaim the good news of God. He came saying, "The kingdom of God has come near," and calling on people to repent and believe (Mark 1:14-15).

2. Apparently Jesus felt that the healing sometimes got in the way of his primary mission. Often, when he healed someone, he told the person not to tell anyone. For example, Matthew recorded Jesus' healing of two men from blindness. Once they could see, Jesus "sternly ordered them, 'See that no one knows of this' " (Matthew 9:30). The two men did not keep quiet about the miracle, however, and "spread the news about [Jesus] throughout that district" (9:31). That sort of news-spreading appears to be why, on several occasions, Jesus chose to leave a town and to move on. After Jesus healed a few people, the sick and injured from the surrounding region flocked to the town. The demand that he stay and heal threatened to overwhelm the announcing of the gospel. Had Jesus remained in one place, healing could have become the sole activity of his ministry.

Mark tells us about a time when Jesus had spent the day in Capernaum. At evening, the sick started coming to him; and he healed many people. The next morning, Jesus went out to a deserted place to pray; but before he was finished, his disciples came seeking him, bringing word that people were looking for him. Instead of going back with them, however, Jesus responded, "Let us go on to the neighboring towns, so that I may proclaim the message there also; *for that is what I came out to do*" (Mark 1:38, italics added).

3. Jesus did not heal every person who was sick or disabled that he encountered. John reported Jesus' visit to the pool of Bethzatha where Jesus healed a man who had been an invalid

for thirty-eight years. In describing the scene, John mentioned that around the pool "lay many invalids—blind, lame, and paralyzed" (John 5:3). Yet, after healing the man with the long illness, Jesus did not move on to the others to see what he could do for them. This again suggests that Jesus did not view healing as his main work.

In the early years of the church, Christians soon discovered that being a follower of Christ was no guarantee of physical healing. The apostle Paul, for example, had to learn to live with his "thorn... in the flesh" (2 Corinthians 12:7*b*-10), even though he appealed to the Lord for its removal. Likewise, the writer of 1 Timothy advised the recipient of the letter to "take a little wine for the sake of your stomach and your frequent ailments" (5:23).

4. When persons with illness presented themselves to Jesus, he was moved with compassion. Three healing stories in the Gospel of Matthew emphasize this compassion. In the first (Matthew 8:1-4), a man with leprosy comes to Jesus and says, "Lord, if you choose, you can make me clean." Jesus responds, "I do choose"; and immediately the man is healed. In the second (Matthew 8:5-13), a Gentile who is an officer in Rome's army asks Jesus to heal his servant who is at home in bed. Without even going to see the man, Jesus heals him. In the third (Matthew 8:14-17), Jesus enters Peter's house and sees Peter's mother-in-law lying in bed with a fever. He, apparently without anybody requesting his assistance, heals her. All these miracles seem prompted by compassion.

5. Despite all the power at Jesus' disposal, he never used it to benefit himself, even on the cross. He never charged anyone for his help. He did not heal to make himself famous. In fact, he tried to keep his healing quiet.

Jesus' work of healing was most plainly seen during the time he spent on earth, plus in the work of his early followers, who healed in his name (see, for example, Acts 3:1-10). In the centuries since, many people have attributed personal healings to Jesus; and since he is a living Lord, there is no compelling reason to discredit such testimonies. Every physician can tell about healings he or she cannot explain. The physician who delivered my first child had a sign in his waiting room that was a testimony of faith. It said, "We dress the wound, but God heals." Still, healings by Jesus in the direct sense of immediate restoration to health are not what we commonly expect, and only occasionally do we witness any healings that we might consider miraculous in the biblical sense.

Learning from Jesus' Healing Ministry

We are able to learn at least three things from Jesus' healing ministry. The first is the significance that many in Jesus' day attached to it—that since he could perform such wonderful and helpful healing miracles, he was indeed the Son of God. John, the writer of the Fourth Gospel, followed that line of reasoning. As one example, John told of Jesus healing the son of an official in Capernaum—another long-distance healing since the son was not physically present. After narrating the healing, John commented, "Now this was the second sign that Jesus did after coming from Judea to Galilee" (John 4:54). John viewed the healing as a sign that Jesus was the Son of God.

Of course, Jesus was not the only biblical character who performed healings. Some of the prophets did, as did some of the apostles. The mere fact that Jesus did miraculous things may be *evidence* of his identity, but it is by no means *proof*. It is not enough by itself to build one's faith on. It is a beginning, however.

The second thing we can learn is that when healing someone, Jesus sometimes linked that activity to the inauguration of the kingdom of God. Recall that the coming of the kingdom of God meant that God was entering human history in a new way that offered new opportunities, new hope, new joy, new ways of thinking, and new ways of living. So Jesus' announcement of the coming of the Kingdom marked the beginning of a whole new era. Jesus was not just one more prophet; rather, in his person, he carried the beginnings of a new realm, the kingdom of God.

One day, Jesus healed a man who had been unable to

speak—which Luke described as casting a demon out of the man. After the healed man spoke, some onlookers said that Jesus' ability to make the demon obey was because Jesus was in league with Beelzebul, the ruler of demons. Jesus responded that if that were the case, the same charge would apply to their exorcists. Then he said, "But if it is by the finger of God that I cast out the demons, *then the kingdom of God has come to you*" (Luke 11:20, italics added). Further, when Jesus sent out the Twelve on a tour to announce the good news, he told them, "The kingdom of heaven has come near. Cure the sick, raise the dead, cleanse the lepers, cast out demons" (Matthew 10:7-8).

Thus, the healing miracles of Jesus in some sense accredit the Kingdom and assure us that the beachhead for this new realm of God has indeed been established on earth. Again, the miracles are not by themselves proof; but they are evidence.

The third and most important thing we learn from Jesus' healing ministry is that by healing the sick, Jesus demonstrated that compassion was one of his primary characteristics and that, by extension, compassion is a primary characteristic of God.

Remember that Jesus came into an age when there was nothing approximating medicine as we know it. To contract almost any kind of illness beyond those that the body could shake off by itself meant that people were doomed to suffer with it without any relief. There were no social services or support groups to help them live with it either.

If you were a healthy person with even a modicum of compassion, your feelings would be assaulted every time you walked down the street. There you would see the blind, the crippled, the diseased, the maimed, and others—all pitifully begging for alms. Your compassion might move you to toss a few coins in someone's cup, but beyond that, there was nothing you could do. So you did what most other unafflicted people did. You tried to shut your feelings down and not to look at the suffering around you.

Jesus, however, refused to closet or protect his emotions and refused to avert his eyes from those who were sick and suffering. Several times the Gospels make statements like these about Jesus: "He was moved with compassion" or "He had compassion on them." For example, after hearing of the beheading of his cousin, John the Baptist, Jesus withdrew to grieve and pray. Somehow the crowds learned where he was and came looking for him. Putting his grief and own needs aside, Jesus "had compassion for them and cured their sick" (Matthew 14:14).

The Greek word for compassion comes from the same root as the word for the bowels, the intestines. That is why we might speak of our emotional response to a sick person by saying, "It tied my stomach in knots," or "I felt it in my gut." Thus, to return to Matthew 8:1-4 for a moment, where a man with leprosy—a horribly disfiguring and disgusting disease if ever there was one, and highly contagious to boot—came to Jesus, we can assume that Jesus had a visceral reaction to this man's agony; he felt it right in the gut. When the man said to Jesus, "If you choose, you can make me clean," Jesus' response was full of compassion. He stretched out his hand and *touched* the leper and said, "I do choose." Do you see what a compassionate decision that was?

Jesus' compassion is good news for us. I am not talking about you and me demanding healing miracles but about how good it is to know that the One whom we have called our Master has, as a primary characteristic, the quality of compassion. That does not mean that he lets us off the hook for wrongdoing without our repenting of it, but it should give us great relief to know that God in Christ feels it in the gut for us and that his first reaction to our woes and the messes we make in our lives is likely to be compassion.

In the 1980s, terrorist groups seeking leverage with the United States snatched several Americans off the streets in Lebanon. One of those taken had been running a school for Arab children. He was held captive for almost four years, half of that time in total isolation and almost always blindfolded. After he was finally freed, he sat for an interview with *Time* magazine. One of the questions he was asked was, "How has captivity altered you?" He replied, "As a hostage, I learned one overriding fact: caring is a powerful force. If no one cares, you are truly alone." [2] That is why it is so important that Jesus was moved with compassion, that he cared. If no one cares about we mortals here on this blue planet, we are truly alone. Thankfully, God in Christ cares about us and has compassion for us.

Following the Example of Jesus the Healer

Jesus' compassion challenges his followers to be compassionate as well. Think about how many hospitals, children's homes, helping agencies, nursing homes, mission-aid centers, rescue missions, and homes for unwed mothers started as the work of churches or Christian groups. Yes, some of them have developed into secular agencies since, but most retain at least some of that sense of following the example of Jesus.

The compassion of Jesus shines brightly in the lives of individual Christians as well, in those who are trying faithfully to follow Jesus' example. Consider Matthew Lukwiya of Uganda, a modern disciple of Jesus Christ who was also a brilliant doctor. He died of the Ebola virus, contracted from patients he treated during a deadly outbreak of that highly infectious disease.

Lukwiya did not have to be in East Africa. He had an outstanding academic record and a medical degree from a good school in Liverpool, England. He could easily have made a comfortable living and had a career almost anywhere, but he felt called to return to his country and to run a mission hospital in Gula.

When the Ebola outbreak occurred, Lukwiya's hospital was the center of the response. After twelve health-care workers died horrible deaths from Ebola, the frightened staff wanted the hospital closed, but by persuasion and the impact of his own example, Lukwiya kept the staff functioning. He imposed strict isolation and infectious-disease procedures, measures that began to corral the epidemic. Then, in a momentary lapse, Lukwiya failed to put on a face shield before treating an infected patient. He contracted Ebola and died two weeks later.

A few weeks before his death, Lukwiya spoke at the

funeral of a nun who had died from the disease. Among his remarks were these words: "It is our vocation to save life. It involves risk, but when we serve with love, that is when the risk does not matter so much." [3]

There is also this story from a 1988 article, and the year is important only because it was a time when doctors had fewer medicines they could use in the battle against AIDS. To have that disease generally meant you were doomed to a short life of suffering and then death. This story was reported in a news magazine and concerned people who opened their homes to take in foster children who were born infected with the AIDS virus. They were the offspring of mothers who had AIDS.

For some of these babies, there was hope. By eighteen months of age, children normally lose the antibodies acquired from their mother. And about half the babies became certifiably HIV negative. When that happened, the babies were removed from the foster homes and placed in permanent situations to make room for more AIDS babies. The babies who did not get better stayed in the foster homes, where they eventually got sicker and died.

Imagine being one of those foster parents—bonding with babies who were either going to die or to be moved out—and then being asked to repeat the process with new sick babies. Talk about needing to have compassion! It would hurt less if the caregiving adults would insulate themselves more—wall off their emotions— and not love the children; but you see, it was the love and compassion that was the redeeming feature for those children. Some of the foster parents even took in the birth mothers when they became too weak to care for themselves.

One of the foster mothers was a Christian named Helen. She was an African American woman described as "a matriarchal blend of sweetness and strength." Helen was caring for twenty-one-month-old Denise, one of the babies who did not lose the AIDS virus. A realistic woman, Helen knew that she would only have Denise for a short while longer, but she refused to detach herself emotionally from the baby. Helen was determined to let Denise blossom into her life for however long the illness allowed.

The reporter described Helen playing patty-cake and singing to the little girl. Helen explained that you "do all those mushy things that prolong the child's life." Here is how the article concluded:

> A few weeks later...the mushy things no longer suffice. The doctors have prescribed morphine for Denise's pain, and Helen has begun to sing, "Jesus loves me! This I know," as she rocks the child. "It's O.K. to go," she whispers. "These arms will hold you again." At the hospital soon after, with Helen and her husband and the birth mother all cradling one another and the child, Denise heeds Helen's sweet voice and dies. [4]

By itself, the fact that Jesus healed some citizens of the first century does not mean much to us. It means a great deal, however, when we understand that he refused to stop healing simply to avoid the pain that caring about others would bring. It also means a great deal when we know that he is now the One to whom we turn. When we add to that the realization of how much good happens today because people are following the example of Jesus as healer, it means even more.

Jesus was moved with compassion. Let us understand that part of being his disciples means that we allow ourselves to be similarly moved.

Study Guide

1. Where have you confronted the view that illness or physical suffering is the result of sin? Can you name any occasions when that assumption might be correct? If so, how should that affect our willingness to care for the sick and suffering?

2. What local institutions can you name that began because of Christians following the healing example of Jesus? How are they supported today? What opportunities do they offer for volunteers to extend the compassion of Jesus to their residents?

3. What healing miracles in body, mind, emotions, or spirit have you personally experienced? What role did your Christian faith and prayer play in their occurrence?

4. How did the story of baby Denise, who died from AIDS, affect you? What did you feel reading the concluding paragraph of her story? How is what you experienced related to being moved with compassion?

6. To be Christian means, by definition, that we are followers of Jesus Christ. Given that only a few of us are called to be health-care workers and that none of us possess Jesus' power to heal, what does it mean for us to be disciples of the Great Physician? How can we follow Jesus' compassionate example?

Notes

1. According to Graydon F. Snyder, writing in *The Lectionary Commentary: The Gospels*, Roger E. Van Harn, ed. (Grand Rapids: William B. Eerdmans, 2001), pp. 188-89.

2. Robert Ajemian, "Terror and Tedium," *Time* (August 27, 1990): 52.

3. "A Vocation to Save Life," *The Christian Century* (March 14, 2001): 5.

4. Richard Conniff, "Families That Open Their Homes to the Sick," *Time* (December 5, 1988): 12-14.

Session 4

JESUS OFFERED FORGIVENESS TO SINNERS

Mark 2:1-12

Some years ago, a sixty-nine-year-old man named William Farley walked into the county sheriff's office carrying a suitcase and his toothbrush. He had come to turn himself in. Actually, the police had not been looking for him, but Mr. Farley had felt hunted for more than forty years—hunted by his own conscience. When Mr. Farley was a young man, he worked at a bank. While there, he embezzled about $6,000. Eventually, fearful that he would be found out, he left his wife and child and for about a year rode the rails, believing the law was pursuing him. Finally, he settled in a town in California under an assumed name. There, he worked as a farm laborer and later in heavy construction and in meatpacking. He eventually married again and fathered three children.

Because of the guilty secret he carried, however, Mr. Farley was never at peace with himself. He said of his new life that he never even had a speeding ticket. "I kept my nose clean and I mean clean," he said.

Finally, after more than four decades with the guilt weighing on him, Mr. Farley went back to the town he had fled and surrendered himself. As it turned out, the local authorities declined to prosecute him. The bank he had taken the money from no longer existed, and the prosecutor said he doubted if any evidence could be found to prove the embezzlement. He added, "Under the circumstances, a mistake that Mr. Farley made [so long ago] should not be held against him after 40 years of useful and lawful living."

When first taken before a judge, Mr. Farley explained, "After living with this thing hanging over my head for 40-some years, it just got heavier and heavier until I just couldn't stand it any longer." [1]

During the days of Jesus' ministry, he had a special compassion for people like Mr. Farley who felt the weight of their misdeeds—a definition that may well have described much of the population of Palestine.

A Symptom of Separation from God

The people whom Jesus encountered daily had heard the strict and legalistic interpretations of the Mosaic laws as explained by the Pharisees, but who could remember them all? These interpretations created a body of requirements much larger than the original laws themselves—such a formidable mass of regulation that only a full-time legal specialist could hope to know them all, let alone live by them. On a daily basis, the common people often knowingly or unknowingly violated one or more of these interpretations. For those who were the most sincere and devout in their intention to be faithful to the laws of Moses, an uneasy conscience must have been a daily companion. No doubt people were exhausted in their efforts to satisfy the demands of legalism. As a community of people, they shared the accusing conscience—and this is to say nothing of intentional sins they may have committed.

A guilty conscience is hardly limited to religious persons, but Christians who try to live righteously find it all too easy to misunderstand Christianity as a series of statements that include the words *must* and *ought*. We say or hear statements that begin, "To please God you must..." or "As a Christian, you ought to..." When we make those kinds of declarations prime directives, we are likely, sooner or later, to feel guilty. In addition, many of us carry the weight of things we have done that are unquestionably sinful—deliberate acts that we know God would not condone.

While we have been speaking of sins that result in a guilty conscience, it is important to acknowledge that Jesus did not forgive sins just to make people more comfortable emotionally. The greater problem with sin is that it separates us from God. Guilt is often a symptom of that separation. It does have one upside, however: it can help us understand that we are sinners and thus make us more receptive to being reconciled to God—something we need whether we feel the weight of our sins or not.

The Incident at Capernaum

One clear theme from the days of Jesus' ministry is that he offered forgiveness to sinners. This theme is especially evident in the incident recorded in Mark 2:1-12, an event two other Gospel writers also recount (Matthew 9:2-8; Luke 5:17-26). While this is a story of Jesus healing someone of a physical infirmity, it includes an added element, one that causes us to view healing more broadly.

Jesus was teaching in a home in Capernaum, and so many people had crowded inside that there was no more room. The crowd blocked even the doorway. Then four men approached the house, carrying on a mat a man with some type of paralysis whom they wanted Jesus to heal. Finding the way into the house blocked, they went up to the roof. The houses of that day were flat-roofed, and the roofing material was usually brushwood covered with clay. Thus it was possible to dig through the roof. That is what these men did, and then they lowered their paralyzed friend down on the mat in front of Jesus. When Jesus saw the man and the faith of his friends, he said to him, "Son, your sins are forgiven."

That response may strike us as odd. Given Jesus' growing reputation as a healer, it was certainly obvious why this man had been brought to Jesus; his friends expected Jesus to heal him. Further, as far as anything in the text tells us, the man on the mat was a total stranger to Jesus, so how did Jesus know he needed to be forgiven? Even more, if it were Jesus' practice to grant forgiveness before he healed someone, then why was that fact only recorded in this particular healing story? Surely this was not the only sinful, guilty man in Palestine.

There must have been something different this time. Somehow, when Jesus looked at this man, he realized that while the man needed to be healed of his paralysis, he had a greater need. If that need was not taken care of, it would leave him paralyzed in his mind and in his relationship with God, even if his body was made whole.

We have no way of knowing whether this man's guilt was deserved. Had he committed some specific blatant sin? Was he feeling the weight of failure to comply with Pharisaic legalism? Was he conscious more than most of the general sinfulness of all humankind? Did he possess an overactive conscience that accused him when no wrongdoing was present? Or possibly, was he possessed by some obsessive emotional state or even mental illness that made him feel chronically blameworthy irrespective of his behavior?

We do not know the answer to those questions, but we do know that the man on the mat was part of a culture where sin and illness were routinely linked. If a person had a serious infirmity, it was generally assumed that it was recompense for personal wrongdoing of some kind. This paralyzed man probably believed that himself. Very likely, he thought he deserved his condition.

In any case, Jesus' response to the man on the mat put the matter in terms of sin. Sensing deep shame in the man, Jesus no doubt knew that in the end, it really did not matter whether that self-reproach was "appropriate" or not. To the man, *his guiltiness felt like a response to sin,* and that was what had to be addressed. Thus Jesus did not say, "Come now, Son. Tell me all about it." He did not urge a public confession or even a private prayer of repentance. He did not counsel, "There, there. You have nothing to feel ashamed about; your guilt feelings do not fit your actions." He did not advise, "You need to forgive yourself." He did not even say, "Your medical situation is not your fault." Instead, Jesus cut right to the cure: "Son, your sins are forgiven."

Jesus' words immediately sparked controversy. Some of those present in the crowd were scribes, professional teachers of the Scriptures. At once, they began muttering to one another, accusing Jesus of blasphemy, saying that only God could forgive sins. We should not immediately fault the scribes; for actually, they were right. Forgiveness of sins *is* God's prerogative. Jews were brought up understanding that all sin, at its root, is directed against God. They knew of the repentance prayer in Psalm 51, where the psalmist says to God, "Against you, you alone, have I sinned, / and done what is evil in your sight" (verse 4). They also knew of the assertion in Psalm 130: "If you, O LORD, should mark iniquities, / Lord, who could stand? / But there is forgiveness with you, / so that you may be revered" (verses 3-4).

Further, their Scriptures taught that forgiveness is a primary expression of God's nature. When the priest Ezra led their ancestors in a national confession following their return from the Babylonian Exile, he prayed, "But you are a God ready to forgive, gracious and merciful, slow to anger and abounding in steadfast love" (Nehemiah 9:17*b*).

As Christians, we are accustomed to thinking of Jesus as a member of the divine Trinity. Thus it is difficult for us to understand the shock the scribes must have felt when he told the man on the mat that his sins were forgiven. At the time of this incident in Capernaum, not even the disciples had grasped Jesus' divinity. Thus, it is hard to blame the scribes for their reaction.

Though the conversation among the scribes was carried on in undertones, Jesus "perceived in his spirit" the nature of these rumblings (Mark 2:8). Rather than argue the point, Jesus pointed to another kind of verification. He said to the scribes, "Which is easier, to say to the paralytic, 'Your sins are forgiven,' or to say, 'Stand up and take your mat and walk'?" In terms of what was demonstrable, saying "Your sins are forgiven" was the easier statement, for where would be the proof one way or the other? Jesus, however, linked the two statements. Explaining,

"So that you may know that the Son of Man has authority on earth to forgive sins," he turned to the man and commanded him to "stand up, take your mat and go to your home." Immediately the man was healed and did as instructed. In other words, the man's sudden ability to walk was proof that his sins had been forgiven. The ability to walk was evidence of an even greater healing.

In Capernaum, with Jesus' assertion of his right to forgive sins, was where the subsequent trouble began. The authorities started to feel threatened by Jesus and got bothered enough eventually to arrange for his crucifixion. It all began with his forgiving the sins of the man on the mat.

The Spirit of the Law

Another incident when Jesus turned to someone and literally said, "Your sins are forgiven" is found in Luke 7. A woman with a bad reputation came into a house where Jesus was eating and started weeping on his feet. She then dried his feet with her hair and anointed them with ointment. The host of the meal, a Pharisee, criticized Jesus for allowing this known sinner to touch him, but Jesus was not dissuaded and said to the woman, "Your sins are forgiven" (verse 48). On that occasion also, those who witnessed the scene were startled by Jesus' statement of absolution. They said, "Who is this who even forgives sins?" (verse 49).

While there are not many recorded instances of Jesus speaking the actual words of pardon, the Gospels are nonetheless full of accounts of Jesus helping people understand what sin is and then giving them the way and the incentive to overcome it. Consider, for example, the Sermon on the Mount, where Jesus elevated the understanding of sin from merely breaking one of the commandments to breaking the *spirit* of the law. We need not kill someone; if we hate them in our heart, we have broken the commandment (Matthew 5:21-22). We need not commit adultery; if we lust in our heart, we have broken the commandment (Matthew 5:27-28). Jesus certainly did not mean that God's laws have no value, but he did mean that the scrupulous attempt to reduce every law to a restrictive set of behaviors without attention to the law's intent misses the point. Unfortunately, some people have understood Jesus' words in the Sermon on the Mount as giving them new things to feel guilty about. They have comprehended well enough that Jesus was enlarging the definition of sin to be not just actions but also attitudes and intentions. At the same time, they have missed the even larger message that "God did not send the Son into the world to condemn the world" (John 3:17) but to save us.

What Jesus Knew

We mentioned earlier that the man on the mat was probably a stranger to Jesus, which leads to the question, how did Jesus know he needed forgiveness of his sins? While we believe that Jesus had the extraordinary ability to know what was in a person's heart, there are also some general things that he knew about all of us.

First, Christ Jesus knows we are all sinners simply because we are human. This is what Paul was referring to when he wrote, "all have sinned and fall short of the glory of God" (Romans 3:23). Jesus made this same point in the incident when a woman who had been caught in adultery was dragged before him with the claim that she should be stoned to death. He said, "Let anyone among you who is without sin be the first to throw a stone at her" (John 8:7). In other words, everybody is a sinner, including the men who were accusing the woman.

This entrenched sinfulness is something no human activity can root out. A story called "The Birthmark," by Nathaniel Hawthorne, illustrates that imperfection is the human condition. In Hawthorne's parable, a doctor is married to a woman of remarkable beauty. She has just one flaw—a small birthmark on her face. Thinking to perfect her appearance, her physician-husband engineered a remedial elixir. He applied the preparation to the birthmark, which did purge the blemish; but the toxin also coursed through her body and took his wife's life. Through Christ, God perfects us without destroying us.

Second, Christ knows we are all sinners through specific things we have done or left undone. One denomination's communion ritual contains a prayer of confession that acknowledges sinful actions, "We have not done your will, / we have broken your law, / we have rebelled against your love, / we have not loved our neighbors, / and we have not heard the cry of the needy." [2] An older ritual puts it, "We acknowledge and bewail our manifold sins and wickedness, / which we from time to time most grievously have committed, / by thought, word, and deed." [3]

We may not be on the run from the law, but things happen that leave us feeling less than good about ourselves. We look at certain situations and say, "I behaved selfishly there," or "I hurt that person and have no chance to correct it," or "I did something really wrong there," or even, "I sinned."

Third, Christ knows that many of us carry unresolved guilt. Not all the things we feel bad about are moral transgressions, and we may be able to chalk some of them up to experience and shrug them off. Still, most people suffer from a guilty conscience occasionally, and often that is deserved. At least a few of the things we have done—but probably more than that— make us feel ashamed or bad about ourselves whenever we happen to think about them because we conclude we were in the wrong. Feelings of guilt, whether appropriate or not and whether related to truly sinful actions or not, can be paralyzing. As Mark Twain's character Huckleberry Finn said about a conscience, "It takes up more room than all the rest of a person's insides."

Fourth, Christ knows that the way to spiritual healing and peace with God is divine forgiveness, not trying harder. The novel *The Rapture of Canaan* by Sheri Reynolds is set in a fundamentalist religious community in the South, in which the pastor controls the life of the people in his church. His flock, having thoughts they are told are sinful, try to distract themselves by putting pecan shells in their shoes and nettles in their beds or binding themselves with barbed wire under their clothing. All these things are supposed to redeem them by making them concentrate on the suffering of Jesus.

While few people go to such extremes, some still try to earn a place in the kingdom of God by piling up good works or by scrupulous living. Good as those things are, they are not the key to spiritual peace and joy. God's forgiveness through Jesus Christ is.

That was a lesson the people of Jesus' day needed to hear, for their attempts to live by all the interpretations of the Mosaic Law often amounted to "trying harder." It was to such people that Jesus said, "Come to me, all you that are weary and are carrying heavy burdens, and I will give you rest" (Matthew 11:28). We who labor at exhausting jobs or who are overwhelmed with other responsibilities may hear these words as a call to find relaxation in Jesus, but Jesus' invitation was not addressed to the work- or responsibility-burdened. He was speaking to those who were trying hard to live holy lives under the tonnage of obeying all the rules the scribes and Pharisees had laid on them. They were the law-burdened.

By comparison, Jesus' burden is light. He did not come to do away with the laws of Moses but to fulfill them by giving them the ultimate construal. In fact, his interpretation can be boiled down to two directives: Love the Lord with all your heart and love your neighbor as yourself.

Faith and Grace

When Jesus announced forgiveness of sins to the man on the mat, he did this on his own initiative with no request from the man. There is more to his action than was apparent, though. Mark tells us that after this man had been lowered through the roof, "Jesus saw their faith" (2:5). At minimum, Mark was referring to the four men who were convinced enough that Jesus could help their friend that they tore open the roof of a house that was not their own. Mark's comment probably also included the man on the mat, however, for he allowed himself to be the centerpiece of this bold move by his friends. It was only after Jesus saw their *faith* that he said to the man, "Son, your sins are forgiven."

Forgiveness of our sins means that we do not have to remain estranged from God because of our past actions. Nor do we have to be paralyzed by the guilty weight of our sins, misdeeds, mistakes, or selfish actions. As this story makes clear, however, it is not simply a matter of, as some self-help books suggest, forgiving ourselves. There is a point where what is usually meant by that advice can be helpful but only after we have first experienced divine forgiveness and, where possible, forgiveness from the persons we may have injured. To forgive ourselves *first* is an ineffectual activity. That is because forgiveness is not the possession of the transgressor to give. If I have hurt you, you may choose to forgive me, but I cannot just say, "Oh well, I forgive myself." Forgiveness is not mine to give. Assuming the person we have hurt is still around and we are able to make contact, we can seek forgiveness from that individual, and we can accept it when offered. Likewise, we can seek forgiveness from God through Jesus Christ and then accept it. Just shrugging off our hurtful action and forgiving ourselves does not deal with real guilt.

To receive that forgiveness, we need faith. In the context of our sinfulness, faith describes, not a mustering up of belief, but the action of openness to receive what Jesus has to give.

We indicated earlier that the scribes were correct when they said only God can forgive sins, which is a way of saying that all sin is ultimately against God. They had not recognized divinity in Jesus and so thought him a usurper of God's right. Still, remembering that God is the ultimate forgiver of sins is helpful for those who live with guilty feelings, especially when the person we have wronged will not forgive—or is no longer around to offer forgiveness. Through Christ, God's forgiveness is available to us nonetheless. There may still be a lot of collateral damage that we have to clean up with those we have hurt, insofar as we can, and there may be consequences that we must pay; but the weight of the guilt can be gone and the chasm between God and us bridged.

That is because the opposite of guilt is not innocence but

grace, the grace of those whose forgiveness we seek and, even more important, the grace of God extended through Jesus Christ. What makes God's grace so generous is that though it is concerned with moral goodness, it does not at all depend on how good or moral we are. God forgives those who sincerely ask. Faith is the acceptance of God's grace.

Jesus the Savior

It is critical anytime we talk about the guilt that we live with to recall what Jesus said about his mission. Most of us can recite John 3:16, but what about the next verse? "Indeed, God did not send the Son into the world to condemn the world, but in order that the world might be saved through him." That verse tells us that moving toward godliness is not a bootstrap operation; that is, we are not told to straighten ourselves up unassisted or to forgive ourselves. Rather, we can count on the grace of God, the unmerited favor and help of God through Jesus Christ.

An old story tells of a man in India who saw that a scorpion had become helplessly entangled in the roots of a banyan tree. Each time the man touched the scorpion, trying to set it free, however, it lashed his hand with its tail, stinging him. A young man nearby laughed at him, "You're wasting your time trying to help a scorpion that can only do you harm." The old man replied, "Simply because it is in the nature of the scorpion to sting, should I give up my nature, which is to save?"

One of the important things we learn from the ministry of Jesus is that it is his nature to forgive and to save. What we need to do is pull our resisting stingers in and, in faith, turn toward him.

Study Guide

1. Some people deliberately do wrong and yet feel no guilt. How would you explain to such a person that he or she needs God's forgiveness?

2. To call some guilt "appropriate" and some "inappropriate" means that while guilt and sin are related, they are not the same thing. How can we test our guilty feelings to decide whether they are appropriate?

3. A lot of advertising conveys the message that we deserve the best of everything—especially whatever the advertiser is trying to sell. How does that message fit with the communion prayer that says, "We have not done your will"?

4. What sorts of nonphysical handicaps may consign people to life on the mat instead of life in the mainstream?

5. Reflecting on the Nathanial Hawthorne story, "The Birthmark," inspired the insight that, "Through Christ, God perfects us without destroying us." What does that mean to you?

6. Are there any sins that cannot be forgiven? Why or why not?

7. Does the fact that not only God the Father but also Jesus the Son can forgive sins have any special meaning for your faith journey?

Notes

1. "Admits Crime 50 Years Later," *The Youngstown Vindicator* (July 23, 1982): 1.

2. "A Service of Word and Table II," *The United Methodist Hymnal* (Nashville: The United Methodist Publishing House, 1989), p. 12. From Service of Word and Table II © 1972, 1980, 1985, 1989 The United Methodist Publishing House.

3. "A Service of Word and Table IV," *The United Methodist Hymnal*, p. 26. From Service of Word and Table © 1957 Board of Publication, Evangelical United Brethren Church © 1964, 1965, 1989 United Methodist Publishing House.

Session 5

JESUS TAUGHT WITH
AUTHORITY

Matthew 7:28-29; Mark 1:21-28;
Matthew 16:13-20

Picture this: While driving through town late one evening, you are pulled over by a police car. The officer tells you he has clocked you driving forty-one miles per hour in a twenty-five miles per hour zone, and you realize he is correct. He then issues you an "invitation" to present yourself at traffic court.

In all likelihood, the experience adds no enjoyment to your evening, but neither does it cause you to challenge the officer's right to issue the summons. Perhaps you could have told him, quite truthfully, that you had not meant to exceed the speed limit, that you had simply been thinking about other things. Perhaps you also could have pointed out, again truthfully, that the street on which you had committed this offense was completely empty and that your speed had endangered no one. Yet you know that neither explanation is a valid reason to break the law.

In other words, you accept that your hometown has the right to establish speed limits within its boundaries and to place law enforcement personnel on its streets to enforce those limits.

Of course, it would be a different story if the officer were not wearing that uniform and driving that car. If he were in street clothes and driving an unmarked vehicle, you would not have immediately acknowledged his authority. That is a way of saying that his authority to enforce the law was a derived authority, not one he possessed by right of birth. He had the right to make traffic stops only because your community's government had empowered him to perform this function. Likewise, your town only had that right because it is a legal entity under the laws of your state, which in turn has been legally sanctioned under the Constitution of the United States—and *that* authority exists because the majority of "we the people" have consented to it.

The opposite of derived authority is direct authority, where a person has power by virtue of who he or she is. There are few examples of direct authority, for most authority is derived. Legend has it that when Henry Ford II was challenged on decisions by people who worked for him, he would sometimes say, "We'll do it that way because it's my name that's on the building." So within his realm, Ford had direct authority, though that was no guarantee his decisions were correct. For centuries, kings claimed to rule by divine right, and autocrats today insist they have similar authority. Sooner or later, though, most of these governments get derailed by democratic movements or other uprisings, proving that even the authority of kings and dictators is not absolute.

Likewise, those of us who are ordained by the church have derived authority. At my ordination, a bishop laid his hands on my head and, using the words of the traditional service, said, "Take thou authority as an elder in the Church to preach the Word of God, and to administer the holy Sacraments in the congregation." [1] The fact that he said, "*Take* thou authority" implied that whatever authority I possess as a minister is derived from the church, which grants it under authority derived from Christ.

The Direct Authority of Jesus

Understanding this matter of derived authority helps us grasp what was going on in the incident early in Jesus' public ministry recounted in Mark 1:21-28. One Sabbath, he went to the synagogue in Capernaum, a town near the northern end of the Sea of Galilee. Mark did not tell us what Jesus taught, but given the usual pattern in the synagogues, Jesus was most likely commenting on Scripture that had been read in the service. What Mark did report was the reaction of those who heard Jesus: They were "astounded," because Jesus "taught them as one having authority, and not as the scribes."

That is a remarkable statement, for the scribes were the Bible scholars of the day, men who had devoted their lives to studying and interpreting the Scriptures. In fact, their predecessors were those who collected, copied, and edited the Scriptures of the Hebrew Bible, putting them essentially into the form in which we have them today. If anybody knew the Scriptures, it was the scribes.

Here came Jesus, however, who, with no scribal training, interpreted the Scriptures in such a way that those listening immediately perceived a stunning difference. The scribes spoke authoritatively about the Scriptures, but theirs was a derived authority built on the work of previous generations of scholars. In explaining Scripture, they quoted predecessors, perhaps citing studies and statistics, pointing out supporting evidence, and offering differing interpretations. Jesus spoke authoritatively as well, but something about the way he talked convinced his audience that his authority was direct, coming from himself in a way that no scribe could match. He quoted nobody and cited no studies. He spoke not his opinion, nor the collective wisdom of scholars, but what he knew to be the truth. He had the authority of an attentive eyewitness who knows what he knows because he has seen what he has seen. Thus, when Jesus spoke, those listening experienced something that instantly agreed, "Yes, of course that is so."

Mark reported that one man present had an unclean spirit. After Jesus spoke, the unclean spirit called out, "What have you to do with us, Jesus of Nazareth? . . . I know who you are, the Holy One of God." Jesus rebuked the spirit and healed the man, but note that something about the authentic ring in what Jesus said enabled this spirit to recognize Jesus' divine identity.

This healing also caused the crowd to once again express astonishment, noting the authority of Jesus' teaching and the fact that even unclean spirits obeyed him.

On another occasion, the crowd who heard Jesus' Sermon on the Mount (Matthew 5–7) had a similar reaction. As Matthew recorded it, "Now when Jesus had finished saying these things, the crowds were astounded at his teaching, for he taught them as one having authority, and not as their scribes" (Matthew 7:28-29).

The Final Authority

This matter of Jesus' authority is critically important when we declare ourselves to be Christian, for that means we accept Jesus—his example, his teachings, his offered salvation—as authoritative for us. Quite literally, *Christian* means "follower of Christ"; thus, he is our authority.

Here's a joke about authority. A nurse was working her first day in a certain Dr. Chegley's office. She was puzzled because the doctor yelled out something every so often—loud enough that everyone in the waiting room could hear. First, he yelled "Typhoid!" Later, he shouted, "Measles!" Later still he hollered, "Tetanus!" This continued to happen with other diseases being shouted, enough so that the nurse began to wonder about the doctor's mental state. Finally, she went to the receptionist and asked quietly, "Why is Dr. Chegley shouting like that?" The receptionist replied, "Well, he *is* the doctor. He calls the shots around here." To be truly Christian, we have to let Christ call the shots!

This is more than stating the obvious. A friend who is a Southern Baptist pastor tells me that within his denomination, there is a battle over what constitutes Baptist orthodoxy. He says that while Southern Baptists affirm without question that Jesus is Lord, there are differing views among them on where the Bible ranks in this matter of authority. The struggle boils down to: Is Jesus or the Bible the *final* arbiter of truth?

The authority with which Jesus taught helps us answer that

question. We are *Christians*, and that is a more important identity than Methodist or Baptist or any other denominational
label. To be a Christian is not at root to be a follower of the
church or a follower of the Bible but a follower of *Christ.*
That is not to say that Christianity is intended to function
independently of the church and the Bible. Both are critically
important in the life of faith; both are places to meet God, and
each has an authority of its own. Nonetheless, the highest
authority for Christians is Christ. As we see in the passages from
Mark and Matthew, the Bible testifies to the centrality of Jesus
and to his authority. It is Christ that gives the New Testament
its power. It is Christ that gives the church its existence. For
Christians, Christ has to be the one calling the shots.

The Authority of Love

We can learn some other things from this matter of Jesus'
authority. For example, because Jesus is the ultimate authority
for us, we can have confidence in the trustworthiness of his
example and the effectiveness of his sacrifice on our behalf.
We can rely on Christ to lead us in the right direction and to
bridge the gap that keeps us from God.

We can learn how to use whatever authority we personally
hold from the fact that Jesus did not abuse his authority. On the
international scene, some who hold authority enforce their will
with armed troops, terror tactics, and other methods of oppres-
sion. On the personal scene, in family life, in the workplace,
and in relationships, some individuals dominate others and
insist on their own way. Theirs is the authority of coercion and
dictation. Jesus has great authority, but his is the authority of
love, persuasion, and invitation, the authority that keeps the
door open for prodigals to return but that does not drag them
to the door.

In fact, Jesus actually refused to do things that would prove
his authority. Clearly, he did not want people joining him only
because their freedom to choose had been overwhelmed by
incontrovertible proof. Recall that one of the temptations Jesus

experienced—and *resisted*—was to throw himself down from the pinnacle of the Temple, thereby making a spectacular entrance and immediately gaining a following (Matthew 4:5-7). On another occasion, some Pharisees asked Jesus to provide a sign to prove himself to them. Jesus refused, saying, "Truly I tell you, no sign will be given to this generation" (Mark 8:11-12).

Authority over Evil Spirits

Recall that in the incident at Capernaum, Jesus exercised authority over an unclean spirit. Can we who claim the name of Christ today be instruments through which Christ exercises authority over the evil spirits of our age? Within both the Catholic and Orthodox churches, there have always been specific rituals for exorcisms. They are not the kind of cross-wielding nonsense shown in horror movies but acts of prayer for persons in the throes of evil. In addition, within all Christian churches, there is a focus on how Christians should confront the evils of the day. Those evils include racial hatred, hunger, torture, abuse, sexism, and so forth. Many Christians have worked under the authority of Jesus to bring an end to such wrongs.

As we confront the evil spirits of our day, it is important that we acknowledge that our authority is derived from Christ. Though we strive to be Christlike, when it comes to authority, we are more like the scribes. We need to acknowledge our scribal limitations but still be channels for authoritative work of Christ. We can have the authority that comes from personal religious experience and conviction, but we need to carefully check our conclusions through the church. One way the authority of Christ is mediated today is through the collective wisdom of the church. Those who claim to act for Christ by killing abortion-clinic doctors are examples of people who assume authority that is not theirs to take.

There are many places where, with Christ's guidance, we should exercise his authority. In a book on prayer, Tilda Norberg and Robert D. Webber argue that there is a need to pray not just for individuals but also for the social structures in which humans live. Those can include families, communities, relationships, workplaces, economic schemes, and other things. Recognizing that social brokenness is a part of the human condition, the authors urge praying for "social exorcism" of those structures. [2]

United Methodist Bishop C. Dale White gave another perspective. When the apartheid system of racial segregation was still in force in South Africa, White and seminary professor Walter Wink were arrested for praying at the White House during a demonstration against apartheid. While the pair sat handcuffed on a police bus, Wink explained that "an act of civil disobedience is not primarily a political act, although it may issue in political change. It is an exorcism! It is a naming of the demons, the first step toward exposing them and stripping away their power to deceive, as Jesus revealed." [3]

We also have demons of our own, though we may not call them that. They can be hatreds we harbor, lusts we cherish, selfish attitudes we do not want to give up, or temptations we toy with. They can be guilty feelings that haunt us, fears that immobilize us, or hang-ups that imprison us. In our prayers, we can ask Christ to help us let him call the shots; we can ask him to exorcise those demons so that we may walk in wholeness and righteousness with him.

We can each, of course, frame our own prayer, but here is one as a model:

O God, like the man in the Capernaum synagogue long ago, I too am troubled by unclean spirits, despairing throughts, and feelings of hopelessness. I often find myself of two minds, caught in the tug-of-war between them. My baser urges are at war with my highest aspirations. Speak your authoritative word of healing. Make my soul whole. Clear my thinking. Tune my emotions. Warm my heart toward others. Cause my demons to depart. Enable me, Lord, to love and serve you with all of my heart, with all of my soul, with all of my mind, and with all that I am. In the name of Jesus I pray. Amen.

The Episode at Caesarea Philippi

While the authority we have as Christians is derived from Jesus, not every authority that was his is granted to us. No single one of us has received the right to define the content of Christian faith and practice without reference to the collective thinking of the church and what it has learned from Christ down through the centuries. One authority that is given to us all, however, is the privilege of "authoring" others into the faith.

We see the beginning of this authority most clearly in an episode at Caesarea Philippi recorded in Matthew 16:13-20. The time was late in Jesus' ministry, after the disciples had been with him long enough to witness many examples of his authority in healing and teaching. They did not know that the days of Jesus' ministry were soon to end, but Jesus did. Shortly, he would begin his journey toward Jerusalem and the cross. Because Jesus understood what lay ahead, he needed to know if his disciples understood what they had been involved in with him. So he asked, "Who do people say that the Son of Man is?" The disciples answered, "John the Baptist," "Elijah," "Jeremiah," or one of the other prophets.

Jesus then asked the question behind the first question, "But who do you say that I am?" Simon Peter, perhaps speaking for the group, responded, "You are the Messiah, the Son of the living God." Jesus then said to him, "You are Peter, and on this rock I will build my church, and the gates of Hades will not prevail against it. I will give you the keys of the kingdom of heaven."

It is in these words that the matter of Jesus' authority comes up. In one sense, Jesus was using symbolism similar to the "keys to the city" concept. In many communities, when an important or famous person makes an official visit, the community leaders present the visitor with a symbolic key. It opens no real door in the city and implies no responsibility for any task in the city. The key is simply an expression of honor. In Jesus' remark to Simon, Jesus honored the outspoken disciple for his faith.

Honor, however, was not the primary meaning of the "keys of the kingdom" remark. Rather, Jesus was giving Simon authority to open the Kingdom to others. Because Jesus' time was short, it was vital for him to empower others not only to speak for the kingdom of God, but also to continue opening the Kingdom doors so that people could enter.

This explains Jesus' pleasure when Simon recognized him as the Messiah. Thus, although the disciple's birth name was Simon, Jesus now called him Peter. It has been claimed that Peter, which means "stone," had not been previously used as a proper name prior to Jesus giving it to Simon.[5] I cannot verify that, but I do know that in Bible times, when a person was given a new name, it often signified a change in function. No longer was this man to be only Simon, the disciple. Now he was Peter, a person authorized to open the kingdom of heaven to others. Jesus would build his church on the rock of faith authority.

If we read only this passage, we might think that this authority was handed to Peter alone. Indeed, these verses underlie the popular tradition—and a host of "pearly gates" jokes—that names Peter as the doorkeeper to heaven. A fuller reading of the New Testament, however, shows that while Peter is singled out here, the door-opening privilege was extended to all Jesus' followers. Jesus' words to the disciples over the subsequent days make it clear that this responsibility of "carrying the keys" to the Kingdom—at least insofar as it means the authority to introduce others to Christ—had been given to them all so that they and those who came after them in the faith could open the doors and let people in. In fact, Jesus' final instruction—about making disciples of all nations—was spoken to the whole group of apostles (Matthew 28:16-20).

As the church spread, the apostles did just that. They introduced others to Christ, who in turn did the same for yet others. The authority to make disciples continues to be handed on today. We, each one of us, have a direct commission from Christ to author others into the faith.

The Keys to the Kingdom

To a degree, the church has institutionalized the matter of authority in the ordination of clergy. Some Christian groups, primarily Catholic, Orthodox, and to some extent, Anglican, speak of "apostolic succession." That term means a direct line of continuity exists between what took place between Jesus and Peter at Caesarea Philippi two thousand years ago and clergy today, a continuity preserved by an unbroken succession of bishops. By and large though, most Protestant churches have not focused on a continuity of bishops but rather on a continuity of message and gospel with the apostles. The hymn "Forward Through the Ages" captures this concept when it begins: [5]

> Forward through the ages, in unbroken line,
> move the faithful spirits at the call divine.

Under either interpretation, apostolic succession ultimately means that what takes place as Christians invite others to follow Jesus is directly connected with this incident involving Peter. The fact that apostolic succession is used in clergy circles as an explicit grant of authority to pastors does not mean that Christian laity do not have a divine commission to share the faith. In fact, that authority to open the doors of the kingdom of heaven is implicit in every Christian's faith.

One reason many pastors prefer their parsonages not be situated next to the church is because they often become by default the keeper of the church key. Most pastors can tell stories about getting phone calls at inconvenient times to go over and open the church. Often pastors handle the matter by making sure that everyone who needs to get into the church is given a copy of the key. In fact, perhaps everyone who joins the church should be given a key right along with their membership certificate.

In terms of our buildings, that may not be practical, but there is a sense in which that is what happens when we declare our faith in Jesus Christ. We may not receive a key to the church building, but we do receive a Kingdom key. Those keys are not to open the Kingdom door for ourselves but to help others enter the kingdom of God as well.

The fact is, however, many of us find it difficult to author others into the faith. Parents sometimes have a hard time using that key with their children. Yet, children are much more likely to embrace the Christian faith when they see it lived out in their homes and hear it spoken of there. We should not rely on the pastor or some church program to spark our children's faith. The church should supplement the home's witness of faith but not replace it. I accepted Christ when I was in my teens. One thing that helped me was hearing the adults around me, including my parents, talk positively about their faith.

We may find it even harder to author faith in another adult. Maybe we have seen some who accept their faith authority become totalitarian in their witness, implying, "Unless you accept Christ exactly in the manner I prescribe, you are not in the Kingdom" or "Unless you believe exactly as I do, you are lost." Such claims misunderstand Jesus' extension of authority. Christian authority is never certainty that our experience of Christ is the only possible one but an assurance that Christ invited us all to himself. The authority Christ gives is never totalitarian. We are stewards of the truth of God's love but never keepers of all there is to know about God.

Authoring others in faith generally does not mean going out and cornering strangers. More frequently, it means using the opportunities that daily living provides to speak a faithful word. I read somewhere about a woman who ate her lunch at the same diner every workday. She almost always had the same waitress; so naturally, they chatted occasionally. The woman was a Christian and that influenced her attitude and spirit. One day, the waitress said to her, "You are always so friendly, and you usually look happy. How come?" At first the woman responded with, "Oh, it's just such a nice day." Then, suddenly realizing the opportunity before her, she said, "A couple of years ago, I had a spiritual experience. I met the living Christ, and I have been joyous ever since." I do not know if that testimony caused the waitress to consider her own faith journey, but the woman who spoke up was doing exactly the right thing. She was opening the Kingdom door a bit and telling of the joys inside.

The act of opening the door to the Kingdom for another person is a deeply satisfying one. Several years ago, the late Sam Shoemaker, a pastor and author from Pittsburgh, wrote a poem titled "I Stand by the Door." He called it an "apologia" (a justification) for his life. In the poem he described his role as a Christian as one who stands by the door of the kingdom of God to show people where the door is located and to encourage them to enter. Here is an excerpt:

The door is the most important door in the world—
It is the door through which [people] walk when they find God.
There's no use my going way inside, and staying there,
When so many are still outside and they, as much as I,
Crave to know where the door is....

The most tremendous thing in the world
Is for [people] to find that door—the door to God.
The most important thing any [person] can do
Is to take hold of one of those blind, groping hands,
And put it on the latch—the latch that only clicks
And opens to the [person's] own touch.
[People] die outside that door, as starving beggars die
On cold nights in cruel cities in the dead of winter—
Die for want of what is within their grasp....
Nothing else matters compared to helping them find it,
And open it, and walk in, and find [God] ...
So I stand by the door. [6]

We can author others into the faith. We can use our key to open the Kingdom door for them. The church is still built only on the rock of faith authority. Without the faithful Kingdom "door opening" of our own age, the next generation will not enter. We do indeed hold the keys to the kingdom of heaven in our hands. We have received them from Jesus himself.

Study Guide

1. What examples of direct authority have you experienced in your lifetime?
2. Where do you see derived authority abused today?
3. What does it mean to you to say, "Jesus is Lord"? In what specific ways is that a statement about authority?

4. How can the authority of Jesus be used to exorcise the "unclean spirits" in our society? What role can we play in that?

5. Think of a specific time you consciously let Jesus call the shots. What was the outcome?

6. Look at the set of actual keys you carry in your pocket or purse. What responsibilities does each key symbolize?

7. What opportunities for authoring others into the faith exist in your daily routine? When have you used your "Kingdom key" to help others meet Christ?

Notes

1. *The Book of Worship for Church and Home* (Nashville: The Methodist Publishing House, 1965), p. 52.

2. Judith M. Bunyi, review of *Stretch Out Your Hand: Exploring Healing Prayer* by Tilda Norberg and Robert D. Webber (Nashville: Upper Room Books, 1999). *Leading from the Center* (Summer Newsletter, 2000), www.gbod.org/leadership/leading/stretch.html.

3. Bishop C. Dale White, *Making a Just Peace: Human Rights and Domination Systems* (Nashville: Abingdon Press, 1998), quoted in *New World Outlook* (September-October 1999), http://gbgm-umc.org/nwo/99so/hbeings2.html.

4. Donald Macleod and J. T. Forestell, *Proclamation*, Pentecost 2 Series A (Philadelphia: Fortress Press, 1975), p. 26.

5. Frederick Lucian Hosmer in *The United Methodist Hymnal*, p. 555.

6. Excerpt from "I Stand By the Door" [Poem by Sam Shoemaker] from I STAND BY THE DOOR: THE LIFE OF SAM SHOEMAKER by HELEN SMITH SHOEMAKER. Copyright © 1967 by Helen Smith Shoemaker. Reprinted by permission of HarperCollins Publishers Inc.

Session 6

JESUS ASSOCIATED WITH BAD COMPANY

Matthew 11:2-19; Luke 5:27-32

In my lifetime, I have been involved with four religious organizations that began because the founder of the organization spent time with bad company. One of these was The Salvation Army, the denomination in which I grew up. The Salvation Army, which is both a church and a helping organization, began in 1865 in London under the leadership of a Methodist lay preacher named William Booth. He saw many churches ignoring the "wrong kind" of people—those with low incomes and no status. So he began making forays into the slum areas of London's East End, talking to people and preaching on street corners. Some who listened to him accepted Christ; but when these converts tried to attend the existing churches, many found themselves unwelcome. Finally, out of necessity, Booth started a church for them and The Salvation Army was born.

Another of these religious movements with which I have been involved (and continue to be) is Sunday school. The first ever Sunday school class met in 1780 in Gloucester, England, an industrial center with a high crime rate. With neither child labor laws nor free public education, most children from the lower classes worked twelve-hour days, six days a week in the factories. On Sundays, their only day off, many of these children simply ran the streets, generally getting into mischief.

About that time, Robert Raikes, a newspaperman who was concerned that so many of the poor ended up in prison, learned that a primary reason many got involved in crime was ignorance of any other way of life. One day, a business errand took Raikes to a rundown part of the city known as Sooty Alley, where he observed several ragged children running uncared for. A neighborhood woman told Raikes that Sundays were even worse, with a horde of unwashed urchins getting into all kinds of trouble. As far as she was concerned, the sooner the children landed in jail, the better.

Raikes, however, decided to try to do something to help these young people get on the right track and to keep them out of the prisons. Eventually, from his own funds, Raikes hired four women to teach the three R's plus hygiene and religion to as many children as he could round up the next Sunday. That was the beginning of Sunday schools. That first effort soon became a movement, spreading to America in 1785.

Yet another religious organization of which I became a part and that started because somebody hung around with bad company is The United Methodist Church. Methodism also began in England, somewhat before either Booth or Raikes were on the scene. In 1738, George Whitefield, an Anglican priest who was an associate of John Wesley, found himself shut out of all the pulpits in Bristol. Whitefield's preaching was so enthusiastic that he drew what his fellow priests considered "the wrong crowd," so they closed their pulpits to him. [1] Finally, he realized that in the nearby community of Kingswood was a whole group of men who never went to church. They were the coal miners, and some considered them "England's worst specimens of humanity." [2] Whitefield went there and ended up preaching to some two hundred miners in a coalfield. After that, he returned several times, each time to a larger crowd.

About that time, his friend John Wesley also found himself shut out of the area pulpits for similar reasons, and so Whitefield told Wesley about the outdoor preaching opportunity—to the wrong kind of people. Wesley took the opportunity, and the Methodist movement was born.

The fourth religious movement with which I am involved is

Christianity itself. Its founder, Jesus, hung around with bad company often enough that on one occasion he was branded as being "a friend of tax collectors and sinners" (Matthew 11:19).

Two Stories from the Gospels

The story in Matthew 11:2-19 begins with John the Baptist in prison. John had previously introduced Jesus by a messianic title, "the Lamb of God" (John 1:29); but now in prison for his unyielding proclamation of righteousness, John wanted to be certain he had identified the right person as the Messiah. Perhaps this uncertainty had been brought on by the depressing gloom of his current circumstances. In any case, John sent his disciples to ask Jesus for reassurance of the latter's messianic identity, which Jesus gave by pointing to his activities.

As John's followers departed, Jesus commented on John to the crowds, using the occasion to praise John. Jesus then pointed out an irony between how he and John fared in popular gossip. John, who lived an ascetic, austere lifestyle and avoided socializing, was accused of having a demon. Jesus, who accepted human comforts and did not avoid social situations, was accused of being a glutton and a drunkard. Even more, some charged, Jesus was "a friend of tax collectors and sinners"; and Jesus did not reject that charge.

It is not hard to understand how Jesus got his reputation, for he spent time with both groups. The story in Luke 5:27-32 is a case in point. One day Jesus saw a tax collector named Levi, sitting at his tax booth. Jesus must have discerned something of value in this man, for he said to him, "Follow me." Levi immediately abandoned his booth and followed Jesus.

Levi then invited Jesus to his house and gave a banquet for him. Levi's friends included other tax collectors and people known as sinners, and when they came to the meal, Jesus sat down and ate with them. Some Pharisees, learning of this, asked the disciples why Jesus did so, implying that to sit down to table with such a crowd of undesirables tarnished Jesus' reputation. We will come to Jesus' response in a moment.

Levi, by the way, eventually became one of the Twelve. We know him better as Matthew, the author of the Gospel that reports the "friend of tax collectors and sinners" charge.

Tax Collectors and Sinners

What made these two groups whom Jesus befriended such outcasts? First, there were those commonly lumped together under the label "sinners." Today we might use this term to describe someone who acts in hateful, greedy, or even criminal ways, but when the Pharisees used the term, they were not merely expressing an opinion about someone's lifestyle. They reserved the word for those whose failure to observe the laws of Moses was common knowledge in the community. Thus, while someone as notorious as an adulterer or a thief would be included in the category, so would the quite respectable man down the street who chose to work on the sabbath, the neighbor who did not attend the synagogue, and the woman who did not keep a kosher kitchen. If we were to translate that category to today's world, it certainly would include some people who behave in conspicuously wrong ways, but it might also include some good citizens who just do not practice any religion.

Second, there were tax collectors (called "publicans" in some biblical translations). Today tax collecting is an honorable profession, but it was not so in Jesus' time because of the way in which the tax-gathering system was structured. Publicans were petty officials of the Roman Empire who collected taxes on salt, duty on goods, and tolls on highways and bridges and any other transaction they could intercept with toll gates or other controls. Rome auctioned the right to collect the taxes, and people bid for the jobs. Those who bid successfully became contract tax collectors. They were authorized by Rome to collect a certain sum from a specific territory in the provinces. They were allowed to keep as profit any money they collected above the contracted sum, no matter how those sums were collected. There were no newspapers and the common people had no way of knowing exactly how much they were required to pay.

So most tax men collected as much as they could. Publicans quickly gained a reputation for malpractice, greed, and hard-heartedness. They were worse than sinners. These were the men who might have had signs reading, "We've got what it takes to take what you've got."

The Jewish people despised all tax collectors, but those tax men who were Jews were especially contemptible because of their legal but unjust extortion of money from their own people as well as their cooperation with the hated Roman overlords. They were considered religiously unclean as well, due to too close contact with Gentiles. Barred from the synagogues by Jewish law, tax collectors were included with things unclean and were even forbidden to witness in any legal case in the Jewish courts.

So tax collectors were hardly well thought of and were singled out by religious Jews for special condemnation beyond that heaped on the common run of "sinners." In the eyes of the righteous, there were sinners and then there were the *really* despised, the tax collectors.

There was this about tax collectors too: They did not have to be outcasts. Rather, publicans were societal outcasts *by choice.* They had selected work that was guaranteed to make them viewed as the scum of society.

If we were to translate this despised category to the twenty-first century, who would be in it? Who are the publicans in our day? Perhaps they are the people making profits through unethical but legally protected behavior, like strip-club operators, porn-shop proprietors, owners of gambling establishments, or certain attorneys who bring frivolous, malicious, or meritless lawsuits to enrich themselves.

The Friend of Tax Collectors and Sinners

To return to the story in Luke 5:27-32, those who accused Jesus of being a friend of tax collectors and sinners missed the point. Jesus associated with these marginalized people, not because he wanted to be one of them, but to invite them to change their ways and to enter the Kingdom. Had the Pharisees been listening to Jesus' explanation, they would have understood that. Here is what Jesus said: "Those who are well have no need of a physician, but those who are sick; I have come to call not the righteous but sinners to repentance" (Luke 5:31-32). His presence with them was not to condone their behavior but to call them into the kingdom of God.

That call was heard. At least some of the tax collectors and sinners with whom Jesus associated changed their ways as a result of that association. If we track this "tax collectors and sinners" phrase in the New Testament, we find three things.

First, the biblical publicans and sinners *listened* to Jesus. As Luke pointed out: "Now all the tax collectors and sinners were coming near to listen to him" (Luke 15:1).

Second, as a group, the publicans and sinners let the gospel penetrate their skepticism. Matthew tells us that even as a result of John the Baptist's preaching, they believed. In Matthew 21, we find Jesus saying to the chief priests and elders:

> Truly I tell you, the tax collectors and the prostitutes are going into the kingdom of God ahead of you. For John came to you in the way of righteousness and you did not believe him, but the tax collectors and the prostitutes believed him; and even after you saw it, you did not change your minds and believe him. (Matthew 21:31c-32)

Third, many of these outcasts took the next step too: They *sought baptism.* Luke reported, "Even tax collectors came to be baptized, and they asked [John], 'Teacher, what should we do?' He said to them, 'Collect no more than the amount prescribed for you' " (Luke 3:12-13).

So after hearing and responding to the good news, these publicans did not remain in their "publicanism." Neither Jesus nor John asked the tax collectors to leave their employment, however, only to conduct it ethically and honestly.

Hearing the Word Today

Now there is something in these stories for us who are inside the church to hear. We know that we can go astray, and when we do, it is good to know that Jesus did not send sinners packing. We understand the sinner part. Sometimes we belong to Sinners-R-Us. Sometimes we belong to Publicans-R-Us, too. We may sometimes do things to drive others away from us, that make ourselves unacceptable to the righteous, or that wall us off from God. In such times, when we number ourselves among the publicans and sinners, it is good to know that Jesus called them and calls us to repentance, and invited them and invites us into the kingdom of God.

We have said that the tax collector is emblematic of those who deliberately choose to be outsiders. As an example, think of a man who joins a hate group such as the Ku Klux Klan. While the man may find acceptance within the circle of the group, he has to know that by joining he is putting himself outside the realm of what most of society considers acceptable. He has made himself a pariah. Yet, Jesus, who ate with tax collectors, came to invite this man into the Kingdom.

Many of us have people in our own families who seem to have chosen the outcast role. The label "black sheep of the family" exists because some people make choices that put them outside the family circle. The phrase became part of our parlance because shepherds disliked black sheep, finding them worth less in the marketplace. Likewise, many people who see themselves as black sheep also feel that they are *worth less* than their siblings or colleagues—or simply that they are *worthless*. Jesus, the friend of outcasts, knows their supreme worth and invites them to the Kingdom as well.

Consider too how many young people seem to go to great effort to be "outcasts." These efforts can range from the fairly innocent to the clearly illegal, from adoption of clothing and makeup styles designed to shock or embarrass their elders to habits their parents abhor to open defiance of adult authority to criminal behavior. While behaviors and choices at the innocent end of the spectrum may be no more than healthy explorations of emerging identity, those further along the continuum can destroy family relationships and set the individual up to be an outcast in significant ways. To these people too, Jesus offers friendship—not to condone their behavior, but to heal.

We do not have to limit our examples to those who get involved with serious wrongdoing, however. Many of us have friends or family members who have chosen other paths besides following Jesus. They may not be doing anything legally wrong but neither are they trying to please God in the way they live. They may belong to the publican-and-sinner category, but we love them and we pray for them. I find it of great comfort to know that Jesus does not write them off.

Table Fellowship

Jesus did not merely talk with people of all sorts; he *ate* with them. Just as Jesus accepted an invitation to dine in the home of Simon the Pharisee—a person of the "right sort"—he also accepted the dinner invitation of Levi the tax collector—a person of the "wrong sort."

At times eating together has an importance far beyond the ingesting of nutrition. My first church appointment was as pastor of a rural congregation in northeast Ohio. There, I was a white pastor serving a congregation that was almost entirely white. There were, however, two black families in the township, one of whom attended our church. In making pastoral calls in the community, I eventually knocked on the door of the other black family and I was welcomed. While there, I invited the family to worship with us. The parents in the home indicated some interest, though they did not commit themselves. They did not come to church the following Sunday nor the one after that, but during the next week, the father called and invited my wife and me to come to their house for supper on a specified evening. We accepted and had a good evening and a good meal together. Subsequently, the family became involved with our congregation.

That was a self-conscious era in efforts to be racially inclusive, and I often suspected that the meal invitation was that family's way of seeing how comfortable we would be in their presence and they in ours. In that regard, that meal together was of high importance.

Likewise for the Jews of Jesus' day. Eating with someone was among the closest forms of intimacy. Luke 14:7-14 tells of Jesus being at the table of a Pharisee and noticing the guests vying for the places of honor, those closest to the host. The reason for this seat scramble was because of how Jesus' contemporaries took the matter of dining together. Who was invited and how near they sat to the host was serious business—as was who was not invited. Jesus went on to advise those listening to him to seek the lowest seats and in so doing, he seems to have accepted his host's table protocol. Jesus just as willingly sat at the table of the tax collector—which was definitely not acceptable by the Pharisee's modus operandi.

I am glad Jesus accepted the indictment that he was a friend of tax collectors and sinners and that he proved it by his actions. You see, I recall people I have encountered in the course of my ministry who simply were not convinced of the value of faith and religion. Some were polite and listened while others made it clear they did not want me to waste their time. One was downright hostile. For many of those people, no matter how many mailings we sent out from the church, no matter how friendly and warmhearted we were as a congregation, it was not enough to break through their resistance to God's call. They were not going to come to worship with us. They were not going to come to our table. I have hope for them, nonetheless, because Jesus said he came not to call the righteous but sinners to repentance. I believe Jesus Christ deals with many such people directly, inviting and welcoming them, just as he did when he was here on earth. We in the church play a role in extending the invitation as well. But for those who, for whatever reason, have no interest in our approach—well, we should not assume Christ is through with them.

The Pharisees

In any discussion about Jesus' association with bad company, the Pharisees come off as hypocritical elitists, and to some extent that is a correct impression. Most were not evil men, however. In fact, they comprised a sect within Judaism devoted to faithfully and scrupulously obeying the Mosaic Law, so their underlying intentions were right. Far from being a conservative reactionary group, they were interested in interpreting the Law for their present day—but in an obligatory fashion. Unfortunately, like many people who succeed in observing the outward expressions of righteousness, some of these Pharisees lost sight of the spirit behind those expressions. Also, although the Gospel writers identify the Pharisees as being among Jesus' tormentors and accusers, we should not assume that every Pharisee felt that way. Remember, for example, that Nicodemus was a Pharisee. He first came to Jesus secretly (John 3:1) but later publicly defended him (John 7:50-51). After the Crucifixion, Nicodemus was in Jesus' burial party (John 19:39). Paul was a Pharisee as well, an identity he apparently kept after his conversion (Acts 23:6).

As a group, the Pharisees were looking for and expecting the arrival of the Messiah. Jesus did not publicly declare himself to be the Messiah, but his rising popularity and his healings led the crowds to begin to consider that he might be the Promised One. The Pharisees, however, could not accept that; Jesus did not fit their expectations. Although Jesus was from the line of the great King David, his personal background and origins were humble. Even worse, Jesus chose as disciples common men with no specialized religious training, including one, Matthew, who was a tax collector. As far as most Pharisees were concerned, Jesus was an impostor.

Thus, even though Jesus' invitation to enter the kingdom of God was extended to the Pharisees as surely as to the rest of the population, many of their number simply could not believe. What is more, many Pharisees put themselves so firmly in the "already righteous" camp that if they had any glimmer that Jesus really was the Messiah, they were convinced they had no need of the invitation.

How we view ourselves in relationship to sin is the point of the parable Jesus told, recorded in Luke 18:9-14. In that story, a Pharisee and a tax collector both went to the Temple to pray (though the latter had to stand "far off" [verse 13] because, as a publican, he was considered unclean and ineligible to enter the Temple proper). The Pharisee's prayer was a litany of self-praise. Thanking God that he was "not like other people," he cited a list of obvious sinners—"thieves, rogues, adulterers"—and his neighbor-in-prayer "this tax collector." Besides stipulating what he was not, this Pharisee listed his spiritual achievements, and without any sense of his own sinfulness, he gained no true sense of God's grace.

The tax collector's prayer was different. He recognized his sinfulness and asked for mercy, and of the two, only he went away forgiven.

The parable helps us see that God views us as righteous only when we recognize our sinfulness and repent of it.

Room for All

Those who branded Jesus as "a friend of tax collectors and sinners" thought there were two kinds of people in the world: sinners and the righteous. What they failed to understand was that Jesus saw only one kind: sinners. We have a choice, however. We can be either sinners or forgiven sinners. Only in the latter group are those who are accounted righteous because of Jesus.

A song called "Carol of the Epiphany" alludes to the kind of people with whom Jesus spent time. The lyrics describe a person seeking Jesus among those who have money and status, only to discover that Jesus lived in poverty. The person then went looking for Jesus in the safest places, those far from crime and trouble, only to discover that Jesus lived in jeopardy. Next, the person sought Jesus among the famous, only to discover that Jesus lived in obscurity. Finally, the person heard where Jesus was—among "those who could no gifts afford." *They* "were entertaining Christ the Lord."[3]

Poverty, jeopardy, obscurity—words all associated with Jesus. On top of that, he refused to disassociate himself with the wrong crowd. What sort of Savior is that?

The right sort, it turns out.

Study Guide

1. What ministries can you name that began through the association of Christians with "the wrong sort of people"?
2. If Jesus were here in the flesh, would he accept a dinner invitation from a Ku Klux Klansman? Why or why not?
3. Who are today's Pharisees? Are we ever among them? How would we know?
4. Besides the examples given in the lesson, who else are today's "tax collectors"?
5. One of the major philanthropists in the area of family planning and AIDS prevention in the developing world has done a great deal of good through his nonprofit organization. In Ethiopia, for example, his program has helped keep the HIV infection rate in that nation's army among the lowest on that continent. This man funds his philanthropy from the profits of his other business, which is one of the largest purveyors of pornography in America.[4] What do you think Jesus would say to this man?
6. Think of a time that you sat down at a meal with someone outside of your social group, someone with whom you would not normally associate. What, if anything, of significance happened as a result?
7. Besides actual meal tables, what other kinds of "tables" present opportunities for associating for the right reasons with "the wrong sort" today?
8. What dangers are inherent for Christians who choose to socialize with today's tax collectors and sinners? How can those be minimized? When should invitations for such socialization be declined?

Notes

1. William H. Gentz, ed. "George Whitefield," *The Dictionary of Bible and Religion* (Nashville: Abingdon, 1986), p. 1107.
2. Basil Miller, *John Wesley* (Minneapolis: Bethany Fellowship, 1966), p. 69.
3. "Carol of the Epiphany," *The Faith We Sing* (Nashville: Abingdon Press, 2001), p. 2094.
4. Jay Cheshes, "Hard-Core Philanthropist," *Mother Jones* (November-December 2002): 68.

Session 7

JESUS WITHDREW TO PRAY

Luke 5:12-16

Two stories about prayer have stuck with me. The first, which I read years ago, is set in the days shortly after World War I and concerns the owner of a small grocery store. In the week before Christmas, a woman came timidly into his store and asked if the grocer would let her have enough food to make Christmas dinner for her children. The grocer asked her how much she could afford. She replied, "My husband was killed in the war. I have nothing to offer but a prayer." The grocer, neither sentimental nor religious, responded sarcastically, "Write it on a paper and I'll weigh it."

To the grocer's surprise, the woman took a piece of paper from her pocket and handed it to him, saying, "I wrote this during the night while caring for my sick baby." Because other customers were watching, he took the paper and placed it on one side of his balance scales. Then placed a food item on the other side. To his surprise, the scale did not go down. So he began to stack more foodstuffs on the scale, but no matter how much he added, the scale did not move. Finally, when he could fit no more on the scale, he said to the woman, "Well, that's all the scale will hold," and he gave her the food. The woman thanked him sincerely and left the store, the bag of groceries in hand.

Once all the customers left, the grocer inspected the scale and discovered it was broken. Yet, it struck him as perhaps something more than a coincidence that it had broken just in time to answer the woman's prayer. He also looked at what the woman had written on the paper. It was, "Please Lord, give us this day our daily bread."

The other story is about a man who met a stranger in a bar. The stranger asked the man, "Do you pray?" "Nah," said the man. The stranger then asked if the man had ever prayed. "Not really," was the reply. "So how much will you take to promise never to pray in the future?" asked the stranger. Thinking he saw an opportunity to pick up a few bucks, the man said, "Twenty dollars." At that, the questioner slapped a twenty dollar bill on the bar; and the man put it in his pocket. After having a drink together, the man left. On his way out of the bar, a wild thought suddenly struck the man. "That must have been the devil. I just sold my soul for twenty dollars!" He hurried back inside to return the money and be free of the promise.

Frankly, when stories put forth their moral that well, I am always a bit suspicious of their authenticity, but I also suspect that, factual or not, such stories convey eternal truths. The truth of the first story is that every sincere prayer has weight beyond the mere words that comprise it. The truth of the second story is that if we have lost the privilege of praying, we have lost something crucial to life itself.

During the days of Jesus' ministry—and right on up to his death on the cross—his practice of prayer demonstrated that he believed both these truths.

Jesus Prayed Often

We cannot help noticing as we read the Gospels that Jesus frequently withdrew from the crowds and often even from the disciples to pray. Also, he usually sought out a deserted place to do his praying. Let me cite a few instances:

- Matthew and John tell us that after teaching a crowd all day and then performing the miracle of feeding the five thousand, Jesus dismissed the crowds and "went up the mountain by himself to pray" (Matthew 14:23; John 6:15).

• Mark reports that Jesus had spent a day preaching and healing people. The next morning, "while it was still very dark, he got up and went out to a deserted place, and there he prayed" (1:35).

• Luke tells us that in preparation for choosing the twelve men who would become his disciples, "he went out to the mountain to pray; and he spent the night in prayer to God" (6:12).

• Luke also tells us that after healing a leper, word of Jesus' ability spread like wildfire and crowds came to be healed. More then ever, his fame grew; and in response, Jesus "would withdraw to deserted places and pray" (5:16).

Obviously, praying was a crucial part of Jesus' life and ministry. The last incident mentioned above, from Luke 5, is especially instructive about Jesus' prayer life. Verses 12-14 tell of Jesus healing a man of leprosy. This news sent crowds thronging to Jesus, clamoring for healing as well. Note, however, what verse 15 does not say. It tells us that the crowds came both to hear Jesus and to be cured of their diseases, but it does not say that Jesus stayed to heal them all. In fact, verse 16 begins with a transitional "but": "But he would withdraw to deserted places and pray."

Given other accounts from the Gospels, there is no reason to think Jesus refused to heal many of the people who came, but with the primitive state of medicine and preventative healthcare in that day, the stream of those desiring a healing touch from Jesus must have been endless. At some point, Jesus chose to turn away and take time to talk with God, his source of strength and power. For Jesus, praying was that crucial.

Commenting on this turning away, Fred Craddock wrote:

> It was no simple or easy matter [for Jesus] to turn away, even for prayer, so long as even one diseased or possessed person asked for help. Some of us regard turning from evil to good a victory; only persons of extraordinary spiritual discernment can at times turn from good to the power necessary to resource the good. [1]

Craddock went on to observe that the withdrawing to pray described in verse 16 is plural. In other words, Luke was not saying that Jesus withdrew from the crowds to pray just on this occasion but that it was a pattern of behavior on Jesus' part, as customary as going to the synagogue on the sabbath.

I recall a mature Christian man of my acquaintance saying that his schedule was becoming extremely busy and that the demands on his time and energy were increasing. "Because of that," he said, "I am taking even more time to pray every day." Human logic might tell us that he should cut down on his prayer time to accommodate more of his responsibilities, but in the logic of Christ, the man's decision to allot more time to prayer makes perfect sense.

Jesus Prayed About Many Things

While, for the most part, we do not know the content of Jesus' prayers, there are enough occasions when Jesus prayed in the presence of others to enable us to draw some conclusions. Here are some of those occasions:

- When asked to heal a man who could not hear and who also had a speech impediment, Jesus looked "up to heaven" and then said to the man, "Be opened" (Mark 7:34). While the words were addressed to the man, the glance heavenward suggests that Jesus was appealing to God for healing power.
- In speaking with his disciples about his impending death and feeling deeply troubled, Jesus posed a rhetorical question, asking whether he should pray for God to spare him from that death. He then answered his own question, saying, "No, it is for this reason that I have come to this hour." Then addressing God, he prayed, "Father, glorify your name" (John 12:27-28).
- At one point, Jesus prayed, "I thank you, Father, Lord of heaven and earth, because you have hidden these things from the wise and the intelligent and have revealed them to infants; yes, Father, for such was your gracious will" (Matthew 11:25-

26). The "wise" may have been the scribes, those trained in the Scriptures but who were unwilling to see the fulfillment of the Scripture in their current setting. The "infants" were then the untutored common people of the land.

- In predicting Peter's denial, Jesus told Peter that he had prayed for him that, following the denial, Peter's faith would not fail. He would return to strengthen his "brothers" (Luke 22:31-32).

- On being taken to the place where his friend Lazarus was entombed, Jesus asked that the stone covering the entrance to the burial cave be removed. Jesus then prayed, "Father, I thank you for having heard me. I knew that you always hear me, but I have said this for the sake of the crowd standing here, so that they may believe that you sent me" (John 11:41-42). The implication of this prayer seems to be to ensure that those who were about to witness the miracle of Lazarus's raising would understand that Jesus was acting with the power of God.

- At the Last Supper, Jesus prayed for his disciples that they might be empowered to carry on with his message and mission after he had returned to God. Jesus' prayer fills all of John 17, but among his petitions were that the disciples would have the joy of Christ "made complete in themselves" (verse 13), that God would protect the disciples "from the evil one" (verse 15), and that God would "sanctify them in the truth" (verse 17). Additionally, Jesus prayed that not only the disciples but also all "who will believe in me through their word ... may all be one" (verses 20-21). Finally, he prayed that those who were given to him would see his glory (verse 24).

- Three of the seven recorded utterances from Jesus while he was dying on the cross were prayers. For those doing the actual work of nailing him to the cross, Jesus prayed, "Father, forgive them; for they do not know what they are doing" (Luke 23:34). When overcome by the despair and horror of what was occurring, Jesus prayed, "My God, my God, why have you forsaken me?" (Matthew 27:46). And as his final breaths where passing, he prayed, "Father, into your hands I commend my spirit" (Luke 23:46).

• The prayer Jesus gave the disciples as a model, that which we call the Lord's Prayer (Matthew 6:9-13; Luke 11:2-4), also informs us about what Jesus considered appropriate subjects for prayer: praise of the Father, the coming of God's kingdom, commitment to God's will, help for daily living, requests for forgiveness and for the ability to forgive others, and strength against temptations.

Thus, from the prayers of Jesus that we do know about, we see that he thanked God, asked for help and strength, interceded for the spiritual well-being of others, and expressed both his agony and his commitment. In short, we can conclude that Jesus prayed about the kinds of things you and I do—the matters of our daily lives, the needs of others, our spiritual growth, our temptations, the things for which we are thankful, as well as expressing our praise of God.

In addition, we know something about the tone of Jesus' prayers. The writer of Hebrews tells us, "In the days of his flesh, Jesus offered up prayers and supplications, with loud cries and tears, to the one who was able to save him from death, and he was heard because of his reverent submission" (Hebrews 5:7). That "reverent submission" was surely the key to the power of Jesus' prayers. That reverent submission led him to pray about his impending death on the cross (which he referred to as a "cup"): "Father, for you all things are possible; remove this cup from me; yet, not what I want, but what you want" (Mark 14:36).

Some of these prayers are from the time of Jesus' life beyond the days of his ministry, after the journey to the cross had begun. Nonetheless, Jesus' life was of one piece. We can assume that the reverent submission that marked his prayer in Gethsemane was a hallmark of his entire prayer life.

Despite all that we can conclude about the content of Jesus' prayers, we are not told exactly what transpired between him and God as he prayed in those deserted places. In fact, that is the point. Most of the time for Jesus, prayer was a private encounter with God. The lesson from that is that our prayers too are primarily for finding our way to God on a deeply personal level.

Jesus Assumed Others Prayed

Another observation we can make from the Gospels is that Jesus did not spend a lot of time urging people to pray. He lived in a culture where most people were taught in the synagogues, as well as by their families, to pray; but it still came down to their own responsibility to do it. As we mentioned in the last chapter, those in that culture who did not go to the synagogues were branded as "sinners"; but there was no real penalty for someone who did not pray. It was a matter of personal duty. Instead of urging people to pray, Jesus assumed that they did.

In the Sermon on the Mount, Jesus did say a few things about prayer—specifically about praying in private and not heaping up empty phrases (Matthew 6:5-8)—but his words imply that he was assuming people were already practicing prayer.

According to the Gospels, the only time that Jesus tried to teach his followers to pray was at their request on the occasion when he gave them the Lord's Prayer. At the same time, he told them the parable of a persistent neighbor who came knocking at midnight, seeking bread to feed a late-arriving guest. The point of the parable was persistence in prayer (Luke 11:1-13). Beyond these few occasions, Jesus simply seemed to assume that people prayed.

Writing a few decades ago about what Jesus told his contemporaries concerning prayer, Theodore Parker Ferris, then rector of Trinity Episcopal Church in Boston, commented:

> [Jesus] assumed . . . that they prayed for their friends. He told them to pray also for them that despitefully used them. Do you see how he began to stretch the area of their prayer? . . . He assumed . . . that they, like us, asked for things they wanted and needed, the necessities of life. He encouraged them to ask, but he went on to tell them, "Your Father knoweth that you have need of all these things before you ask." Ask, but be brief in asking. And the implication is, go on to other things, greater things, beyond your own little needs. [2]

Thus, if we are going to follow Jesus, praying is a necessary activity. The assumption is, "You are a Christian, so of course you pray."

Jesus Prayed in Deserted Places

Mostly, what Jesus gives us about prayer is his own example, which, much of the time, was to withdraw to a deserted place to do it. That practice tells us a couple of things.

For one thing, it suggests that we need to be intentional about finding time for praying and listening. It does not have to be an hour at a time, but there needs to be that purposefulness about our prayer life that keeps it from being forgotten or neglected.

For some people, prayer does not have to be at a specified time or in a quiet place. In the seventeenth century, a man named Nicholas Herman joined a Carmelite monastery in Paris. His name was changed to Brother Lawrence, and he was assigned to kitchen duties. He found he could pray there as he did his work. Brother Lawrence wrote, "That time of business does not with me differ from the time of prayer, and in the noise and clatter of my kitchen, while several persons are at the same time calling for different things, I possess God in as great tranquility as if I were upon knees at the blessed sacrament."[3]

Another thing about Jesus' practice of praying: it behooves us to think about where the deserted places in our lives are. For most of us, deserted places do not refer so much to physical locations as to parts of our lives where we forget to invite God. I read an article once by a woman who had a long commute by car to her job every workday. She said that the one hundred minutes she spent in the car each day seemed mostly wasted time. Then one day, while fretting over how haphazard she had been about allotting time to pray, it occurred to her that she had such time in the car, and she began using it. Obviously she did not shut her eyes or try to read the Bible, but she did turn off the radio and laid out before God the things that were on her heart. She did not spend all her time in the car that way, but she said she found an enrichment of her spiritual life beginning to take place.

Deserted places can also refer to places where we lack what others have. Not much is known about William Walford, who, in 1842, wrote the words of "Sweet Hour of Prayer." We do know that he was a minister who lived in England and that he was totally blind.[4] Maybe this hymn grew out of his experience with living in a world where the ability to see had deserted him. Our places of lacking may not be physical, as his was. We can encounter emptiness where we lack joy, peace, contentment, love, or some other inner quality.

Further, deserted places can refer to times where we suddenly feel alone because of temptations or rage or discouragement or doubt or some other inward experience. That sense of aloneness was illustrated in the 1983 movie *The Big Chill.* It told the story of a group of people who had been friends in college gathering for the funeral of one of their cohorts who had committed suicide. Confined to a house in the country, they renewed acquaintances, had occasion to view the course of their lives since their college days, and discussed what had become of their idealism. Clearly they were troubled that the departed, the one whom they had considered most talented among them, would take his life. In the conversation, the friends explored how their lives and friendships had been reinterpreted in the context of their grief, shock, and life experience. In a particularly poignant exchange, one friend stated, "Wise up, folks. We're all alone out there, and tomorrow we're going there again."

Those friends were discovering deserted places in their lives. We all have some, and filling them with prayer—if only a brief call to God—can change the complexion of the experience in a way that brings us more in line with God's will.

A few years back, the late Jacques Maritain, a Catholic philosopher, wrote a letter to a seventeen-year-old girl. We do not know her identity, but apparently she had been raised in the church. Then she found herself in a deserted place where, because of something that happened, she felt she had lost God. She was left angry, and she wrote to Maritain about it.

In writing back, Maritain told her that things would not always look to her as they did at that moment. He appealed for her to use every ounce of her intelligence and suggested some things to read. Then he added:

> I am not telling you to wait, I am telling you rather to take advantage of the fact that you are completely broken and beaten to the ground in order to set yourself to a real search for truth—putting

your childhood behind you.... I am not telling you to wait—*I am
telling you to pray* as best you can, blaspheming perhaps, groping and stammering. Tell [God], "If you exist, make yourself
known to me." [5]

At any time when the forces of existence weigh upon us so
that we feel we are in a deserted place, we can and should pray;
but that is not all. The example of Jesus shows us that prayer
should be part and parcel of our lives all the time. Then, when
we get to those bad spots, we are not getting reacquainted with
God but turning to the one who has been making himself
known to us all along. Under those circumstances, even in
deserted places, there can be sweetness in prayer, whether it is
the prayer of an hour or of a moment.

Prayer and Personality

The point of studying Jesus as a person of prayer is not
only to understand more about him but also to find principles
to apply to our own life of prayer. That said, we ought not to
assume that prayer is a one-size-fits-all pattern. Our goal is not
to reduce Jesus' prayer life to a template we must follow stu-
diously. God has made us as individuals and we cannot assume
that we can or even should all pray in similar ways. How we
pray and to some degree what we pray about will differ
according to our personality.

I thought of that recently when I was paging through the sec-
tion of a hymnbook titled "Prayer, Trust, Hope" looking for a
hymn to go with the topic of prayer. Prayer was the subject of a
sermon I was planning to preach, and so I paused when I came
to the hymn "Sweet Hour of Prayer." In the hymnbook I use when
preparing the bulletin, I note in the margins the dates that we have
used each hymn, in order not to pick my favorite ones too often.
At "Sweet Hour of Prayer," however, there were no dates noted
on the page. I have been the pastor of the church for more than
seven years, so that meant that in all that time, I had not selected
this hymn for one of our services.

I wondered briefly why I had not used the hymn. It has a

singable tune that just about everybody knows, and its message is certainly a good one. Why had I been avoiding it? I considered that perhaps it was because of the word *sweet*, which strikes a different emotional chord today than it did in 1842 when Walford penned it. Then, it denoted something valuable, whereas now it has a maudlin sound to it. Most of us probably would not use that particular adjective about prayer. Yet, many of our hymns come from earlier eras and contain words used in poetic but noncontemporary ways. So that was not the reason I had not selected it.

Finally, I decided that it might have something to do with the word *hour*. Yes, I know that the expression "sweet hour of prayer" does not mean literally sixty minutes spent praying. It is used figuratively to mean something like "a refreshing time of prayer" and refers more to the act of praying itself than to the amount of time doing it. Still, that *hour* word seems to trip me up.

As a young person growing up in an evangelical denomination, I heard lots of sermons that urged us to spend lengthy times praying—some said that an hour a day was hardly enough—and that we should set a certain time apart each day and spend it in prayer. Seeking to be a faithful Christian, I tried many times to do it. Each time, it instilled a sense of dread in me about the experience. In the first few minutes, I had pretty well said to God everything I had on my mind and then I would sit there trying to listen for what God might be saying to me but not experiencing anything I could identify as "spiritual." Finally, always well before the designated time was up, I would leave, feeling frustrated.

I eventually understood that I was trying to fit myself into a prayer mold that does not come in a standard model. For me, prayers that seem to connect are generally brief and uttered at various times throughout the day, often while in the midst of other things. I tend to hear God best through reading and study. Other Christians find that different forms of prayer work better for them.

The point is that however we do it, we need to pray. We need to come before God, voice in some way what is on our hearts and minds, and then find the ways that work best for us to listen.

Prayer has great weight. It is crucial for our lives. Jesus believed in and practiced prayer and so do his disciples.

Study Guide

1. What deserted places in your life could benefit from prayer? Why?

2. What do you make of Maritain's advice to the seventeen-year-old girl that even blaspheming in prayer is better than not praying?

3. Regarding our own needs, Theodore Parker Ferris interpreted Jesus' teaching to be "Ask, but be brief in asking. And the implication is, go on to other things, greater things, beyond your own little needs." In what circumstances are even our big needs "little"? When should we linger longer in prayer over our own needs?

4. Recall a time when you received an answer to prayer. How did you know it was God's response and not coincidence?

5. What form of prayer or pattern of devotional life seems to best connect you to God?

Notes

1. Fred B. Craddock, *Luke,* Interpretation: A Bible Commentary for Teaching and Preaching (Louisville: John Knox Press, 1990), p. 72.

2. Theodore Parker Ferris, *What Jesus Did* (New York: Oxford University Press, 1963), p. 45.

3. Brother Lawrence, *The Practice of the Presence of God,* Douglas V. Steere, ed. (Nashville: The Upper Room, 1950), p. 24.

4. Gordon Avery, *Companion to the Song Book of The Salvation Army* (London: Salvationist Publishing and Supplies, 1961), p. 174.

5. Martin Marty, *Context* (February 1, 1983), quoted in the newsletter of St. John's Episcopal Church, Youngstown, Ohio (April 1, 1984).